MW00855645

The Garment of Praise For the Spirit of Heaviness

God bless
Darlene

McDougal & Associates
Servants of Christ and Stewards of the
Mysteries of God

The Garment of Praise for the Spirit of Heaviness

by

Darlene Graves

Published by:

McDougal & Associates
18896 Greenwell Springs Road
Greenwell Springs, LA 70739
www.ThePublishedWord.com

McDougal & Associates is dedicated to the spreading of the Gospel of Jesus Christ to as many people as possible in the shortest time possible.

ISBN 978-1-940461-48-9

Printed on demand in the U.S., the U.K. and Australia
For Worldwide Distribution

Dedication

I would like to dedicate this book to the love of my life, my late husband, Dale Graves. He was absolutely a gift from God. Every family should have a husband and dad like him. He was my wisdom, my direction, my protector, and I cherished him for all he gave me and for the wisdom he left me with. My prayer is that all can find a spouse who can become their second half.

When Dale died, I sought for someone to take his place, but there was no one who could fill that void except Jesus. He has now become my Protector, my Director and my Wisdom. I want to praise my Father in Heaven for giving me forty-six years with a man who chose to love his family unconditionally and left us all with so much understanding.

I would also like to dedicate this book to my beautiful children, grandchildren and great-grandchildren and to all the wonderful people Father God has put in my life to make me who I am. It is because of Gods grace that I have come to know Him and that I have learned to love those around me with unconditional love.

Contents

The Spirit of the Lord God is upon Me,
Because the Lord has anointed Me
To preach good tidings to the poor;
He has sent Me to heal the broken-
hearted,
To proclaim liberty to the captives,
And the opening of the prison to those
who are bound;
To proclaim the acceptable year of
the Lord,
And the day of vengeance of our God;
To comfort all who mourn,
To console those who mourn in Zion,
To give them beauty for ashes,
The oil of joy for mourning,
THE GARMENT OF PRAISE FOR THE
SPIRIT OF HEAVINESS;
That they may be called trees of righ-
teousness,
The planting of the Lord, that He may
be glorified."

Isaiah 61:1-3, NKJV

Introduction

In a prophecy given to me at an Aglow foot-washing service conducted on 2/27/1996, God said:

So many hurts, so much of the dirt from the earth. But you I bring today. I wash that dirt from you. I pour my love into your wounds, that you may be healed. Yes, I love you with a love unmeasurable. You cannot measure the love that I have. My children don't realize how much I love them.

I call you this day to come higher. Come higher into My presence. There were only three that I took to the Mount of Transfiguration. The others were not ready to come. I revealed Myself to them. Come, my daughter. Come to that higher place and enjoy the revelation of My love, My heart for you, that you may be healed and you may obtain the blessings that I have even for those who cannot come into that secret place.

They are bound, bound by the bondages of the earth, but you can come, My daughter, and obtain those blessing for them. Come up higher. Come up higher this day, My daughter. I love you so! I love you so!

The Lord anoints your ears afresh, that you may know the will of God. As you walk in newness of life, as you study His Word. He will show you what you're to do. You are not to worry. He will confirm the Word with signs following. He will confirm the Word by those around you, counselors, those who know the Word. So do not fear, My daughter. Those things that you see in the Word. He will confirm it.

The Lord anoints your hands to touch those in darkness with the mercy of the Lord, mercy pouring forth from those hands. Those who sit in darkness, they don't know they've never seen the mercy of the Lord. But you hear their problems, you lay hands on them and take that sin and lift it up to me, that My mercy may pour forth and cleanse them, cleanse them of their sin.

A holy calling ... This is a holy work. The Lord anoints your feet to walk in paths of darkness, bringing the light of My Gospel, salvation to those who don't know Me, who have never heard. How can they hear without a preacher? I send you forth this day, preaching the Word, preaching My Word, giving My light, giving My mercy.

I see the heartbreak of the women, as I saw them in the fields.

Introduction

These were amazing words to hear for a woman who had suffered so much in life. I had gotten off to such a bad start and then made so many wrong turns along the way. But God is so gracious and merciful to us all. He can turn things around for us and even give us *The Garment of Praise for the Spirit of Heaviness.* This is my story and I trust that it will encourage and bless many who are even now in the throes of despair. There is hope. His name is Jesus.

Darlene Graves
Conowingo, Maryland

Chapter One

In the Beginning
(My Childhood)

When our life begins, we have no say in it. We are simply a complex creation of a Supreme Being I have come to call Father God. Before the world was created He knew us and created us to be His precious friend.

Unfortunately, because of the choices made by Adam and Eve, we are all born in sin and formed in iniquity, and there is no good thing in us. That is why God had to send His precious Son Jesus Christ to pay the price for our sin, so that we could be forgiven and given new life.

When Father God created us, He gave us the ability to make choices. He didn't want to create robots; instead, He wanted a people who would love Him and want to follow Him, and who would also love the people they were put in contact with. Because of Jesus, we can choose to walk in forgiveness, and we are given a second chance of knowing peace, joy and forgiveness through obedience.

I was born to a set of parents I did not choose, and they would not have been my choice. Nevertheless they were exactly the parents who were needed to make me who I was intended to become. When Father God created me, He not only knew me, but He knew what I was to accomplish in my lifetime.

I was born in Baltimore, Maryland in 1937, to a mother who was an alcoholic and a father who was a gentle, beautiful man with patience beyond measure. Dad also had the gift of wisdom. For instance, one day, when I was a junior in high school, I remember going to him and telling him that I wanted to quit school. He responded by saying, "That's fine, but let me give you something to think about: if you quit school now, you will have lost eleven years of your life. You only have one more year, and then you will have something to show for it." I thought about what Dad had said and decided that he was absolutely right. I completed my high school, graduating with an academic diploma.

There was a reason for Mom's alcoholism. She was emotionally ill. Seven years prior to my birth, she had given birth to a son, but that son only survived for two weeks. I have always believed that his death caused Mom to become emotionally unstable.

Mom's doctor was also partly to blame. He suggested to her that she drink a couple beers in the evening to relax her. She obeyed this orders, and her couple of beers escalated until she had become an alcoholic. The drinking, of course, did nothing to resolve her emotional issues. It only caused more problems.

When my brother I never knew was born, Dad was working in a funeral home, and Mom blamed him for bringing home germs that had killed their baby. She never got over it and was never able to walk in forgiveness, so she became lost in a world of anger, resentment and hostility.

Needless to say, Mom didn't know the Lord. She didn't choose to know the Lord, and therefore she didn't know how to get free from her anger. Instead, she chose to stifle her emotions in a bottle, and that led to her alcoholism.

Unfortunately, when tragedy comes to our lives, all too often we rationalize away the circumstances, we try to fix them ourselves, or we run from the reality of what is happening and hide in some habit. The real answer would come in turning to the Lord and seeking His help. What a simple solution! The Bible teaches us, *"My people are destroyed from lack of knowledge"* (Hosea 4:6).

When people don't know the Lord, they fall into bondages and, unless someone helps them, they remain in those bondages. The Lord offers us many resources to help us regain our freedom. For alcoholics, there are programs like AA, NA, Celebrate Recovery and many others. Due to the fact that we are mortals, we usually prefer to walk by our own understanding and what we are feeling, and therefore we become our own guide. Generally, our feelings lead us into a state of self-pity, and that leads us into negative emotions, and then we turn to something that can take the pain away.

When we come to know the Lord, we have the help of the Holy Spirit and are able to see much deeper into our actions and their consequences. Jesus Christ died so that the Holy Spirit could come and convict us of our sins. He sets out to reveal the truth which is hidden deep within our spirit or our inner man.

Our soul is made up of our mind, will and emotions. Therefore, when we don't deal with our inner man, we try to cover the pain with an instant cure, by turning to drugs (including prescription drugs), alcohol, sex or something else. Then our hurts, hang-ups and habits become our master, which causes us even more problems. The result is that we lose our money, health, feelings and relationships, and then we begin to blame others. This, we mistakenly feel, will help us with our escape.

Our marriage begins to fall apart, our parents become sick from worry and fear, and one-by-one our children fall into the same rut we have already established. As long as we continue to walk this path, there is never an answer. This explains why my own life became unmanageable and unbearable, I had very low self-esteem and was unable to make good choices on a day-to-day basis.

In the Beginning

When I was still living at home, Mom would often tell me that I was stupid, I was ugly, and I would never amount to anything, and, like so many others, I came to believe her words. How unfortunate that parents fail to understand how their actions and their words cut into the heart of their children. Why is it that they cannot seem to understand that these little people are the building blocks for the next generation.

My problems went beyond poor self-esteem. I was born with crippled feet and bad eyesight. My grandfather, whom I called Grandpop, lived on Baltimore Street (in Baltimore City), and he had an artificial limb shop. There he made me some special shoes.

The first pair of shoes Grandpop made me were not very nice to look at, but they helped me walk better. Later he made me some special arch supports that I was able to put into my store-bought shoes. These weren't much better to look at, but eventually I was able to graduate to orthopedic shoes. Because my shoes looked strange, the other children in school would make fun of me, and this just added to my insecurities.

I was not without some spiritual guidance. As a youngster of ten, I would walk by myself to a Lutheran church every Sunday. Dad would give me money to bring home some doughnuts and a newspaper. I found comfort in the doughnuts, and they became my addiction. Throughout life, I had a hard time eating just one doughnut. Once I got started, I couldn't quit. Much later in life, when I began to learn about addiction, I came to realize that I could not go into a doughnut shop and purchase a dozen doughnuts. I would eat them all before I could stop myself.

My parents didn't go to church, but Mom always made sure my sisters and I were baptized as infants in a German Lutheran Church in Baltimore. The service was all in German, so I never really understood what I was hearing, but it didn't matter that I didn't understand. There was something different in the atmosphere there, and I was drawn to the calm presence I felt.

At the age of twelve I began attending a Confirmation Class. The pastor taught us on the book of Job, and when he got to the place where Job's wife told him to curse God and die, I became oppressed by a spirit of fear and was tormented by it for the next thirty years. When I approached Mom and told her about my bad dreams and bad thoughts, she went to find her Bible and read from the book of Job, trying to understand what I was telling her. Her conclusion was that what I was telling her was "stupid." She told me that all I had to do was forget about it, and it would go away. But it didn't go away, so I sought other ways to fill my inner self.

One day Mom brought home a Ouija Board. It became my best friend, and I found it quite exciting to play with. I also liked reading my horoscope. I didn't realize how evil and dangerous both of these pursuits were. To me, it was fascinating and exciting, but I was totally unaware of the negative world I was getting involved with. As usual, I was looking for something to make me feel good about myself.

Across the street from Grandpop's artificial limb shop were shops where people told fortunes. They covered their windows with heavy blankets, and I found that to be quite intriguing. This made me even more curious about the occult. I never actually dared to go into one of those shops; just the thought of what was going on inside them was frightening enough. However, my fascination with them led me to become possessed with witchcraft.

When I was seven, my sister Leslie was born. Until then, Mom had walked me to school, but now I had to walk with another mother in the neighborhood who took her children to school. One day, I was late, and this lady left me. I decided that I could get myself to school. When I got to the bottom of my street, a very nice-looking, blond-haired man approached me in his car and asked if I wanted a ride to school.

I said, "No."

He told me he had something nice in the car for me to play with, but something about that man made me very fearful, and I ran for my life. I found places to hide, on neighborhood porches and behind bushes, until I finally saw him go by.

When I got to school, I told my teacher about this experience, and the teacher called the police. The next thing I knew I was on my way to the police station, and I vividly remember having to stand before a group of men in a lineup. They had the man who had tried to lure me into his car handcuffed to the men on either side of him. When I saw those handcuffs, I got confused, and it became very difficult for me to pick him out of the lineup. It seemed to me that the whole line of men were bad, and I was very frightened standing in front of them. I never knew what happened to the man, but I never saw him again.

In a more general sense, life in those days was very good, and most of my memories were also good. For instance, I never forgot the milkman delivering milk to our house. When it was cold, the cream at the top of the bottles would freeze, and my sisters and I would eat it with a spoon.

I also remember Dad being bitten by a dog while he was working. For some days, he lay at home very sick with a fever. Mom was pregnant at the time with her fourth child, Leslie had measles, and I had whopping cough. Mom handled that difficult situation remarkable well. She was Nurse Nightingale, and it was one of the few times I really respected her.

World War II came, and there were periodic blackouts in our neighborhood. At night, I would look out past the window blinds and see men walking up and down the streets with flash lights, guarding our homes. It was a very frightening time. Food was rationed, and everyone was having a hard time being able to live a normal life.

Another good memory was that every Saturday night Mom would take me to the movies. After the movie, we would stop at a neighborhood bar on the way home. She would get beer and fried hardshell crab. I would play darts with the men in the bar and eat the dough off her crab. I always looked forward to this experience because it seemed to be one of the few times Mom and I were able to enjoy doing something together. When small children have very little, they cling to the most simple experiences.

On one of these outings, on the way home, I fell. As a result, I got blood poisoning in my leg, and the infection went all the way up to my hip. For two months, I sat soaking that leg. I was told that if the infection reached my heart, it would kill me. That was another difficult and frightening time.

As my sisters grew, it seemed that they could do no wrong. Whatever happened was always *my* fault. When they wrote on the dining room wall with crayons, it was my fault for leaving the crayons lying around. When they wrote on the dog with my lipstick, it was my fault because I had left it lying where it didn't belong. Mom may have been right in these cases, but because I was already suffering from the inability to like myself, this just made my self-hatred all that much worse. It also caused me to dislike my sisters.

Blaming others is so easy, but it surely makes life hard. If only parents would come to know the Lord and express His wisdom and love to their children, they could grow up to know and understand the beauty of God's love instead of the hatred the devil brings to us.

When I was twelve our family moved from Baltimore to Maryland's Eastern Shore, and life changed dramatically. Dad was made the manager of a dairy in Salisbury. This should have put us in a different standing in the community, but when people learned that we lived in a trailer, rejection was, again, part of my life. As a result, I wasn't well accepted by my peers in Salisbury either.

Trailer living was only recently becoming a way of life in Salisbury, and we were among the first to live in one of these mobile homes. Some people judged us as "trailer trash," and life continued to be difficult for me.

Dad had long belonged to the Masons and Mom, too, was an Eastern Star, so they convinced me to join the young adult group in Salisbury. My stay in that organization, however, was only a few months long. I was not well received, and the experience only heightened my problem of low self-esteem. I was to find acceptance only in a local church youth group, but that's another story, one that I will get to presently.

The mobile home park we lived in was quite small, only ten to twelve homes. We had a family of Gypsies come to live in the park. They told fortunes, and again I was drawn into the negative spiritual world. One night there was a bad storm, and seven trees fell over the Gypsy king's trailer. Amazingly, however, the trees fell on each other, and not one of them touched the home. When they were later removed, the mobile home hadn't suffered even a scratch on it. This amazed us all.

One of the young Gypsy boys became attracted to me, and one night he took me out. We parked, but when he approached me to have sex with him, I said "no." I got out of the car and started walking home. He respected me for that, and so he apologized and took me home. Our friendship went no further.

When I was finally old enough to drive, one night Dad let me borrow the car. I picked up one of my girlfriends, and we went to the movies. Early the next morning, when Dad went out to get in the car and go to work, the car caught on fire. He accused me of smoking in the car. Later he learned that the wiring had been bad and that's what had cause the fire. He apologized for having wrongly accused me. As a result, my love and respect for him only increased. He was a truly wonderful man.

Another time, I went to pick up a friend. After turning into her driveway, a man stopped and told me to come down to the end of the driveway, that he was going to kill me. I was terrified and ran into the house for safety. My friend's dad went out to deal with the man and came back to tell me that the man had been drunk and was a little crazy anyway.

One November morning, it began to snow very hard, and I asked Mom if I could stay home from school. She said no. I got ready, and she drove me to school and let me out at the front door.

I watched until she had left, and then I decided to leave too. I really didn't know where I was going or what I was going to do, but I just didn't want to spend the day in school, when most everyone else was staying home.

As I walked, before long I met a friend, and we walked together. Then one of our male friends came along in a car and asked if we wanted to go to the ballpark and slip and slid in his car. We agreed, and we had lots of fun that day.

But then someone called the local radio station to say that school would be closing early that day. Hearing the announcement, Mom called the school to say she was coming to get me. When someone went to give me that message, I was nowhere to be found.

When we got back to school that day, I was called into the principal's office. "So where have you been?" he asked.

I told the principle that I had decided to take a walk, but I didn't tell him about my friends who accompanied me. He reprimanded me and told me not to do it again, and with that experience, I discovered that it was always best to tell the truth.

I didn't believe in lying, but I hadn't thought that not telling the whole story was actually a lie. What I had done, however, was deceptive, because I hadn't told the principle about my friends. That experience left an impression on me that I never escaped. I learned that day that no matter what you do, it is important to own up to it. At the same time, however, I began walking in denial by protecting others when they were wrong. This, I was to learn, is called codependency, and I personally suffered from codependency for many years afterward.

I had learned one good lesson that day. When you do something wrong and then lie about it, you only compound things and make them worse. It's a principle I've tried to convey to my children and, later, my grandchildren.

Since I had always found such great comfort in going to church, I decided to join a local Baptist church and began associating with the young people there. It was there that I truly found acceptance for the first time. One day I asked one of my new Baptist friends how you can know when you should go down the aisle and accept Christ as Savior. "You'll know," she said. Sure enough, one night my feet took flight, and I found myself at the front of the church. I gave my heart to the Lord and was soon baptized in water.

When Mom learned of my intention, she didn't understand why I had to do this when I had already been baptized as a baby. At this point, however, I really didn't care what she thought. She and I didn't have a good relationship, and I was convinced that this experience would set me free from the torment I had been enduring. So, I forged ahead with my plan, and, as I expected, the moment I was baptized, I felt cleaner than I had ever felt in my life.

Being baptized had been right, but my motivation had been wrong. God didn't want me to just do the right thing; He wanted my heart. Too often we rationalize away our problems, not choosing to really deal with them. I didn't understand that I was dealing with an evil force. I knew I had a God who was good, but I didn't know or understanding that the devil was alive and well and how much power we give him because of our ignorance of his ways.

I also didn't realize how much God loved me. Because I couldn't see Him with my natural eyes, I believed that I was in control of the circumstance of my life, and I continued to play the blame game to cover my mistakes. At the same time, I chose to create in my mind a place where I could hide and no one could see me. This was my way of protecting myself from other people's offenses and accusations.

Dad was the only stable element in my life. When Mom would go off on her tangents, I would lose my sense of direction. I rebelled against her, but the love and character my father displayed created conviction in me. His love and understanding always made me want to do the right thing.

At one point, I bleached my hair in the front, and by keeping it wrapped up for the next three weeks, I kept Mom from seeing it. When I finally did let it down and she saw what I had done, she immediately turned to

Dad and said, "Dick, did you see what she has done? What are you going to do about it?"

Dad said, "What would you have me do, Margaret? It's already done." Because his response was one of love, I became even more convicted of doing things I shouldn't be doing.

I remember Mom being so angry that she threw dishes at Dad, and still he did not respond. Instead, he sat quietly in a chair and tore at a paper he had in his lap.

One day Dad did react to these provocations, and I thought he was going to kill Mom. I grabbed him by his legs, to hold him back. When he finally got hold of himself, he left and went to his office at the dairy. I got on my bicycle and rode there to comfort him. I sat at his feet and wept. The result was that Mom accused me of trying to break up their marriage.

My one joy in life was dancing. On Friday nights I would go to the Baptist gathering hall, where we would have jitterbugging. On Saturdays I would attend square dances, and on Sunday nights I would go to the skating rink, where we would do ballroom dances on skates. I was a pretty good skater, and I never had a problem getting a partner. What did life hold for such a messed-up teenager?

CHAPTER TWO

My Young Adult Life

After graduating from Wicomico High School in Salisbury, I went to visit Grandpop and Aunt Sis, who now lived in Parkville, Maryland. The first week I stayed with them, I was able to land a job with the C&P Telephone Company. When I called Mom and told her I wouldn't be coming home, she surprised me by being okay with it. My sisters later told me that Mom was very proud of me and would tell everyone how well I was doing. I just wished she had spoken more positive things to me while I was still living at home, instead of always belittling me. Anyway, now I had a new life.

I rode the streetcar to and from work and, again, had an encounter with a perverted man. He would get on the trolley and sit with young, single women and attempt to rub their chest with his elbow. One day he got off the trolley at my stop and tried to follow me home. I ran and hid behind a tree alongside the house next door, and, in the process, discovered a good looking young man who lived there. He saw me and came out of the house to see what I was doing in his yard. I told him I was hiding from a strange man who had followed me when I got off the trolley. What a strange way to start a wonderful relationship, one that lasted the rest of our lives.

To finish with the story of the perverted man: He followed my cousin's girlfriend home and then attacked her, leaving her behind a bush for dead. She and I went to the authorities, and the man was caught and punished.

The name of the young man I met while hiding in his yard was Dale Graves. He was very handsome and very personable. He was a strong willed man (which is what I had lived with all my life), so I was immediately very comfortable with him, and we hit it off quickly and started seeing each other regularly.

When I got an opportunity to go to Washington and try out for a play, Dale told me I had a choice to make: I could either go to Washington or I could stay in Parkville and date him. Insecurity and uncertainty made me choose to stay in the relationship with Dale. To me, the relationship with him seemed like a sure thing, but, as a result, I never found out what might have happened if I had chosen to try out for that play.

So often we make decisions by what we feel, and things don't turn out well for us. Then there are times when, after we have thought things through, we are sure we have come up with the right answer, but still, the situation doesn't turn out as well as we would like.

We need to pray and ask for direction from God. He never steers us wrong. Even though I didn't do that, God had his hand on my life, and the decision I made was the right one.

Dale and I began to date in the summer of 1955. When Christmas came that year, he gave me a watch. I was disappointed because I had thought I was going to get a ring. Then, on his twenty-first birthday, February 23, 1956, he took me out to dinner. That night he pulled a little box out of his coat and gave me the engagement ring I had been longing for. He had already proposed on the front porch of my aunt's house. Kneeling down, he asked me to marry him. I said, "Are you sure? I don't believe in divorce. This will be a lifetime commitment, and I will never give you a reason to divorce me." He said he agreed. We were married on September 1 of that year.

As Mom and I stood in the second floor bathroom of my aunt's house, looking out the window and watching Dale get into his automobile, all dressed in his tuxedo, I was thinking how handsome he was, but Mom was her usual self. "Look at him," she said, "you know he'll never amount to anything." I couldn't believe what I was hearing. Why would she say such a thing? Those hurtful words crushed me, and when I was walking down the aisle an hour later, it was with unnecessary insecurity and confusion. Once at the altar, I didn't know whether to say I do or to run away.

If Mom's words were not enough to spoil our special day, on the way to the church, the limousine I was riding in went down a one-way street the wrong way, and when the driver made a U-turn, the door in the back where I was sitting flew open, and I almost flew out. When we did get to the church, the preacher was twenty-five minutes late, and the church attendant couldn't speak English. Dale wasn't sure what was going on. In the end, by God's mercy, it all worked out, and I was at peace. I knew I had made the right decision, and it was this relationship the Lord used to change my life.

Married life is never easy, and it took a lot of hard work on both our parts to make a go of it, but we did. We had only been married about three months when Dale's best man, who was also his best friend, came to the house one day and tried to proposition me. I wouldn't let him in the house, and I told Dale about it when he got home from work.

Dale called the man and told him he was no longer welcome in our home and to never come back there again. It is amazing how a situation like that can be a positive element in a relationship. This was what God used to teach both of us to trust each other. It was the beginning of a relationship built on trust and communication (even though I was sometimes a Jezebel and tried to manipulate my husband).

There were times when we made stupid decisions. For instance, on our first anniversary, Dale went out with a friend in a little boat we had purchased, a big storm came up, and he almost drowned. When he came home, instead of me being angry with him for spending our first anniversary on that boat with a friend, I was just so glad I hadn't lost him altogether.

We had been married two years when our first child was born. We named him Dale, Jr. and called him Frankie. Frankie was born on July 28, 1958. I was at the end of my term, my water had broken three days before, and when the baby kicked, I was so dry I could count his toes. He was a stubborn little one, even before he was born (and he didn't change much as he got older).

Eventually, the doctor had to induce my labor, and when Frankie was born his little head looked like a purple cone. Nevertheless, he became a beautiful young man and was very bright. He was a born leader. Unfortunately, neither Dale nor I had the foresight needed to train him in that area and his talent was used negatively.

When he was still an infant I would walk him around the neighborhood in a scooter — whenever the weather permitted — and talked to him constantly, pointing out all the things there were to see, telling him about animals and what they would say, and pointing out the various colors. As often as possible, Frankie and I would join a group of my friends and their little ones on walks for the same purpose. By ten months, he was already able to put together whole sentences.

The Garment of Praise for the Spirit of Heaviness

One night I had put Frankie to bed in his crib, and a storm came up. After a big strike of lightning, he stood up in the crib and said, "Did you hear that? What that was?" It was very exciting to have our little one, not only be able to recognize and name things, but also to put together words and make sentences, even before he could walk. This may sound strange to modern-day young people, but in those days, we didn't have all the electronic gadgets now available to help children learn.

On June 28, 1960 our precious daughter, Darla Marie, was born. Frankie and I had gone for a two-hour walk, and when I got to the doctor's office, he found that I was dilated five centimeters and should have been in hard labor. He asked me if I was having any discomfort, and I told him no. He asked me to wait for him in the waiting room, and when he called me back into the office, he sent me right to the hospital. Darla was born forty-five minutes later.

I had experienced difficulty carrying her, but we never expected that she would die when she was just two weeks old. She was born with neonatal-anemia. Unfortunately, medical science had not progressed as much as it has today, and the doctors didn't know to transfuse the baby when she was born. They sent her home to die, and we were not made aware of what we were dealing with.

Since I never had labor pains with any of my pregnancies, I was never aware when my babies were ready to be born. After the seventh month, the doctors would have to check me every week, to see if I was dilating. It was very strange, and poor Dale thought he would surely have to deliver at least one of the babies.

We brought Darla home and thought we had the perfect family. Who would believe that our precious baby would be dead in two weeks? She died on July 10, and I didn't handle her death well. I went back into a place I had created in my mind as a child and, at times, became suicidal. I would sit in the living room with Frankie and watch him get into mischief and only by God's grace did he remain safe. I was in some other world at the time.

There was a Lutheran Church next door, and one day I took Frankie, and we went over there and knocked on the door. I asked the pastor if he could help me and explained that I was very depressed because of the death of my baby. He was wonderful.

Frankie and I sat in the pastor's office, and he told me a story of a preacher who had lost his entire family. They had all been killed suddenly, all at the same time. The preacher had become very depressed and had a hard time handling the situation. Then, he said, several months later, the preacher was driving down a road and found a young child lying on the side of the road. He picked up the young child and took it to his town and founded an orphanage. Instead of him becoming bitter, God was able to use his horror and turn a negative thing into something positive and beautiful.

What the pastor shared with me that day made a lot of sense, but my grief was too new, and I still wasn't able to find peace.

Dale decided he would start a business and so, within two months after the death of Darla Marie, he and Frankie and I were on our way to starting a new life. This seemed to be the perfect solution. My tendency had always been to run away from my problems. I had been a runner all my life. Unfortunately, the problems always went with me and would surface later down the road in another way. Somehow I just couldn't run away from myself.

Dale decided to move us to Salisbury. Since I had lived there during my teenage years, I had a wonderful friend there I had known a long time. Dale and my friend's husbands got together and decided to start an automobile upholstery shop. There was none in the area. The problem was that starting this new business caused Dale to be away from home more than usual, and I became even more unstable and depressed as a result.

We had rented a house on the outskirts of town, near an overpass. One day I decided to go for a walk with Frankie. We walked up onto the overpass, and as I stood and looked down at the railroad tracks beneath the overpass, I became overwhelmed with the thought of jumping. I didn't want to die; I just wanted to show people what a horrible person I was. All my life my mind had been filled with negative thoughts. I had now been tormented by a spirit of fear for four-teen years, and God had taken my little girl. *Surely*, I thought, *I wasn't worth much*. But as I looked down on the tracks beneath me, and then I looked at my little two-year-old, I realized there was no way I could do that. I would either have to leave him on the overpass, or I would have to take him with me, and he didn't de-serve to be hurt. I went back home, but I continued to be depressed.

The Scriptures say that God never gives us more than we can endure without giving us a way of es-cape (see 1 Corinthians 10:13). When Dale came home from work that night, he found me huddled in a corner next to the refrigerator. I told him I was going to die and said to him, "Please love your next wife." Dale was a wonderful man, and it's hard to know how he put up with me. Thank God he was chosen to be my husband. Within three weeks, I learned that I was pregnant with baby number three, and that was the spark I needed. Our God is so good. He gave me something to live for.

Some Jehovah's Witnesses began to come to our house, and I started to study with them. For the mo-ment, they represented Christianity to me, but when they told me I couldn't have the baby I was carrying transfused (if it should have some blood problem), I began to doubt everything else they had been telling me. Since I had attended a Baptist church as a teen-ager, I called a local Baptist pastor, and he began to come by and teach me the Bible. The Jehovah's Witnesses would come on Wednesday, and the Baptist preacher would come on Thursday. He would discuss with me the information the Witnesses were leaving behind, and I decided I couldn't believe what they were telling me and asked them not to come back anymore.

Dale and I found a new home to rent, this one closer to the business, and I began to sell home interiors. One day, as I was standing in our dining room practicing my sales presentation, an automobile ran into the side of the house. It hit the house so hard it threw the concrete blocks of the basement wall across to the other side of the house. The man who was driving died a few days later from an aneurism in the brain.

The blocks that were thrown across the basement crushed Frankie's little play car. Thank God he wasn't playing down in the basement at the time, or he could have been crushed as well. By now Frankie was a typical two-year-old boy, and he liked to jump into the bed. One day, as he was diving into it, his head hit the window sill, and I had to take him to the emergency room. He needed stitches in his forehead.

Several weeks later Dale purchased a swing set for Frankie and set it up in the backyard. Frankie and a little friend were playing on it, and the friend pushed the swing and clipped Frankie's eyelid. It bled so much that I thought he had lost his eye. He hadn't, but someone in the hospital decided that I must be abusing my child and had me checked out by the authorities.

On the one-year anniversary of Darla's death, I went to the hospital to have baby number three. We named him William and called him Billy. He was born with bacteria in his bowl, and again I lived in fear. He suffered from this bacteria for a full year.

Of all my babies, I wanted to hold Billy more than the rest. After the last baby had died, I had felt a pain in my arms that just wouldn't go away. But Billy was a very independent little fellow and wanted nothing to do with cuddling.

Then, suddenly, we had a new crisis. The man Dale had gone into business with started bringing ladies to the business in the evenings. Dale didn't want to tell me about it because he knew how unstable I was at the time. Instead, he decided that he should give the business up and move us back to Harford County. He sold the new business to his partner for two $2,000 and an antique truck. I'd had no idea all of this was going on, and it came to a head very suddenly. Although I was pregnant again, with baby number four, up the road we went to find a new life.

When we got to Harford County, we were able to rent a suitable house right in the town. Frankie was more active than ever now, and he decided to play with a bee's nest by pounding it with a stick. Bees got down into his shirt, and so many of them stung him that he went into shock. We had to rush him to a doctor, and he was given a shot of Benadryl. Thank God he survived it.

When Billy was given sulfur for a cough and a high fever, we had no idea that he was allergic to the drug. He turned blue, and we had to rush him to the Johns Hopkins emergency room. They rubbed him down with alcohol baths until he cooled down and turned a normal color.

Next, Frankie got the measles. Dale had never had measles himself, and he couldn't afford to get it because he had just opened a new business. Billy was only a year old, and we didn't want him to get sick too. And I was pregnant again. We all had to have preventive shots.

The man we were renting from refused to put heat in the house, and when September came, and it began to get cold, we decided to move again. This time, we moved into an old inn. It was very eerie and appeared to be haunted. We only stayed there three months, and then we were able to rent a property that had a house and a separate building Dale could use for his business. It was located on Bel Air Road in Fallston, Maryland. We stayed there for nearly thirty years.

We moved into that home on Bel Air Road at the end of November, and David, our fourth child, was born on December 27. When I went to the hospital, I was given a room next to the nursery. During the night I heard a nurse and doctor talking about an infant who was having breathing problems. When morning came, my child was not brought to me to be fed. I questioned the nurse, and she said that my child was "too young" to be brought out of the nursery.

"That's not true," I told her. "I know better. This is my fourth child. Tell me, was it my child who had breathing difficulties during the night?"

When she didn't answer, I hopped out of the hospital bed and went to look through the window of the nursery to see for myself. What I saw broke my heart. My little boy's body was being heaved into the air every time he exhaled. I left the window hysterical and told the staff, "I want my husband, my doctor, and my preacher. I don't care in what order. Get them here. Just do it!"

Dale was the first to arrive, and he came in just as the doctor was going by the door. Having learned of the problem Dale's face was gray, and I wasn't much better. As I sat on the bed and looked out of the window, watching smoke billowing out from the smokestacks onto the roof, it looked like angels dancing on the roof. I began to pray and tell God, "I can't do this again. Please, Lord, I can't lose another baby."

Then a thought came to me: *the baby will live.* I didn't know where that thought had come from, but it didn't seem to matter. I just started claiming it as my own.

The doctor came in next and told us the baby didn't have any fluid in his lungs, but that he still had no more than a twenty-five percent chance of survival.

I chose not to believe him. Within twenty-four hours David began to breathe on his own. He was a miracle from God.

When the preacher came the next day I told him, "My son is healed."

He said he would have the church pray for us anyway. "You cannot have more than enough prayers." We brought David home ten days later and began to see the hand of God at work. The Word of God shows us that what the devil means for harm the Lord will turn to our good (see Genesis 50:20).

David suffered some more. He had a ruptured navel, and when he was six months old, he got pneumonia. Then he became allergic to milk, and we had to put him on a special diet.

We suffered in other ways. When David was three months old, the woods in back of our house caught fire, and the fire came all the way to the edge of the house. We survived it all and raised our children in that house until they were grown.

Chapter Three

The Early Years of Our Marriage

The next five years were fairly normal. Dale and I struggled to raise three little boys on an income of $10,000 a year. Just keeping up with three boys kept us on our toes.

There was a creek that ran down the center of our property. The house was on one side of it, and the business was on the other side. We built a bridge to drive over to the business and then, about twenty feet up the creek, we built a foot bridge to be able to walk between the house and the business.

Frankie was a piece of work, and when he was about five, he decided he was Tom Sawyer. He built a boat out of boards, tying them together with heavy cord, and then tried sailing his creation down the creek. He was gone for hours that day, and I was not aware of what he had done or where he had gone. When he didn't come back, I took our dog Duchess and a switch and went looking for him.

When I finally found Frankie, he was soaked to the waist. "Where have you been," I demanded?

"I was floating my boat down the creek," he said, "and it sunk, and I got all wet. I didn't want to come home until my cloths had dried."

I said, "Frankie, don't you know better? You are wet, and it is cold out here. You could have gotten sick."

All the way home I flicked him on the bottom with my long switch and fussed with him. "Frankie," I said, "you are restricted for a month. Don't even ask to go anywhere."

One day Dale gave Frankie a shovel and told him to do a job for him. Frankie went and found five more shovels and then five little boys to work the shovels. If only he had used his leadership ability for good instead of wasting his life on drugs! When he was eleven and started to use drugs, he was just as aggressive with that as with everything else he had done in life.

He was a mathematical genius. When he took the national mathematics test in his senior year of high school, he came out in the top 3% in the nation. I sometimes looked at this beautiful man, with such a mind, and wondered what Dale and I could have done differently to inspire him. In time, I came to understand that an attitude of addiction begins way before the problem is visible. Children need to be tempered and taught obedience. Dale and I didn't understand the drug world and the deceptive ways it worked; therefore we were ignorant to see what was happening right in front of our eyes.

In later years, as Jesus sent me out to work with broken people, I saw the spirit of addiction a lot, and I noticed that it started in little people. Now that the Lord has opened my eyes, I am able to see the over-bearing spirit that causes our youth to try to control the people and circumstances around them. We, as parents, become frustrated and lose our ability to temper them. Then the children control us and learn the art of addiction.

Dale and I also didn't understand the spiritual world, so we couldn't see what was happening in that unseen world. We were so busy trying to control our circumstances. If we had only sought understanding from the Lord, how different our life would have been!

Because we have been given the ability to reason, we miss the opportunity of walking in obedience by seeking God's wisdom. Instead, we choose to learn obedience through the things that we suffer. If *we* fail to learn obedience, then we pass down our mistakes to our children and our children's children.

Unfortunately, too often we allow the attitudes we have acquired in childhood to control us, and this destroys our marriages, our businesses and our children, as well as our own lives. We first need to walk in forgiveness toward ourselves, for allowing our lives to go to the devil. We need to forgive God for not stopping us from our mistakes. And then we need to forgive whomever we have chosen to blame for our misfortunes.

Billy, the second boy we raised, was also very special to us. (Personally, I don't believe we ever have children who are not special." If God made anything better, He kept it for Himself. His word says that we must come unto Him as a little child, for they represent the Kingdom of God (see Matthew 18:1-4).

As I noted earlier, when Billy was born, I so wanted a child to love, to take the place of the little one I had lost, but he was very independent from birth. He wouldn't even let me hold him to feed him. After Darla Marie died, my arms ached to have another baby to hold and to love. This wasn't in my mind. The pain was real.

Billy was different in other ways. He didn't talk until he was three. He would stand in front of the refrigerator with his arms folded and wait, and Frankie would shout, "Mom, Billy wants milk." Billy didn't have to talk, it seemed. Frankie did it for him.

One day Frankie came in the kitchen and said to me, "Mom, if Billy is playing in a puddle, will he get wet?" I wondered how he could be playing in a puddle because it hadn't rained for three weeks. I went out to investigate and discovered that the wooden top of our septic tank had rotted and fallen into the tank, and Billy had found a long stick and was playing in the raw sewage. Oh my, thank God he didn't slip in, for he never would have been found. Ironically, Bill now runs the Harford County water purification plant.

As a boy, Billy also enjoyed playing with bugs. The bushes in front of the house were full of praying mantises, and he loved to play with them. We didn't have many spiders.

Billy would fall asleep almost anywhere. One day I found him sleeping in a toy box — with the lid down. Another time I found him asleep in his little kiddie pool. We had a convertible, and when we would go for a drive, Billy would stand up in the back seat, hold on to the support, and go to sleep — even when the top was down.

David, our third son, was interesting in his own way. He would go out under the trees in the front yard and build small towns. He was very shy and withdrawn and didn't mingle well with crowds. Unlike his brother Frankie, he was a follower, but, sadly, in time David also became an addict.

David was a sleep walker. One night, after putting all the little people to bed, I was sitting in the living room, and I heard water running. I went to investigate and found David standing in the utility room relieving himself in his father's shoes. I also found him trying to blow the pilot light out in the furnace. Such an interesting child!

One day the Lord spoke to me and said, "If you want order in your home, you must get rid of the confusion." Do we teach our little ones to organize, or do we take care of all their wants? It is important that we teach them to take care of their own personal things. But, because we don't want them to have to suffer as we did when we were young, we stand in the way of them learning obedience through the things they must suffer.

Too often, because we have never learned how to say no to them, we teach our children to manipulate others to get what they want. It is so important for us, as parents, to teach our children how to earn what they want and need, rather than just supplying them everything.

As he grew up, David became a manipulator and would push and push until he finally got his way. One night he pressed my last nerve, and I became so angry I picked him up and pressed him against the wall. After that, I decided I would never correct David again; I would let his dad do it. I didn't realize I had so much anger in me.

Five years went by, and I became pregnant with our fifth child. She was due on August 7 but wasn't born until September 1. Donna was born on our 11th anniversary, at precisely the same time we had walked down the aisle to be married. God couldn't have given us a better anniversary present. Oh, how we cherished that child!

But Donna became the hardest of our children to raise. We tried to protect her from everything, and I walked in fear of losing her. As a result, I suffocated her with my protection. When I discovered, many years later, that I was codependent, I also discovered that I was my children's worst enemy. Dale was also codependent, so our children got a "double whammy."

My codependency stemmed from the emotional abuse I suffered as a child and my inability to forgive my mom. Dale's dad had walked out on his mom before he was born, so his Grandmom and his aunt had raised him on a farm. They did the best they could, but he was given too much freedom and very little direction.

Then, when Dale was fourteen, he went to live with his mom, and his step-father wasn't very understanding and patient. He must have resented the fact that Dale had come into his life, so one day he chased Dale out of the house with a butcher knife. Soon Dale became involved with the wrong group of young people, and he began to steal cars and ended up in the a reform school at the tender age of sixteen. This became the family secret.

How sad! Our children could have learned from our mistakes, rather than having to make the same mistakes themselves. Dale wouldn't tell our children about his past and wouldn't let me tell them either. Also his mom had prevented him from seeking out his real father or from getting to know his other siblings. Our children reaped the whirlwind.

In time, Dale and I were able to purchase the property on Bel Air Road for $25,000, the property with the creek running through it. Several years later, when the county allowed the local hospital to be built upstream of us, the new lay of the land caused heavy runoff to come our way. The ground was not able to absorb it, and it would run into our creek and periodically flood our property, and those floods destroyed our business.

The building Dale used for the business would flood so badly that he had to erect some high shelves on which to store the rolls of upholstery material he kept on hand. In time, when the state created the floodway map of the area, they used our property on Belair Road as a marker. Consequently we were not allowed to build anything else on the property or to improve it. And we also could not sell it.

It got worse. The house was on one side of the creek and the business on the other, and the creek began washing away the foundations of the house and undermining it.

When we had purchased the property, the house only had two bedrooms. Needless to say, it became very difficult to raise four children in a two-bedroom home, so we decided to create another large bedroom in the attic. While we renovated the house, we moved several miles away and rented a house in the Bel Air area.

A person never understands why they do the things they do or is able to see what the future holds for them. The renovation of the house was not just because we needed a bigger home; the Lord had a purpose far greater than anyone could have ever imagined at the time. When the renovations were done, we moved back to the property.

One day, as I was making the beds in the upstairs, the Lord spoke to me and said that the property was going to sell for $200,000. I laughed, just as Sarah had when she was told she would have a child at the age of ninety. Who would believe that the property could sell? I said, "This property is condemned. This must be You, Lord, because only You could pull that one off." It didn't happen right away; it actually took several years before it came to pass. God had much to teach us before He could bless us.

Our life stayed very simple. Our boys were typical boys, and our little girl was a princess living in a house with three boys. One day, when Donna was two, I looked out the kitchen door and saw her playing in a concrete trough filled with water. I asked her what she was doing. She turned to me and said, "Mom, I won't eat them." I went out to see what exactly was in that trough. It was filled with rain water, and in the water were lots of developing tadpoles. Donna was pinching them and watching them jump.

Oh my! Raising a little girl with three big brothers was not easy. She would do some really interesting things: like standing in front of the potty and thinking she could tinkle in it just like her brothers did. She would really get upset when her little legs got wet.

Donna grew up protected by the boys, but in the process, she became very tough and wouldn't let anyone into her heart. She was also Daddy's little girl. I tried to protect her, but my relationship with her was based on fear. It was very hard to see what was happening, not only to our daughter, but to our sons as well.

Father God saw my problem, but I was blind to it. I was not able to break through the wall I had placed around myself ... that is, until I chose to walk in forgiveness toward my own mother. Before God could free me from fear, low self-esteem, and everything else I had acquired, I had to first forgive her. Father chose an interesting way of freeing me from my dilemma, but this didn't happen until many years later.

Since Dale restored vans and upholstered them, many young people were drawn to our home, and we formed a club for them — a van club. Dale was the leader, and we all went on van trips and also had van parties in our yard.

One Christmas, we all went to the mall and did a collection of canned goods, toys and money. We also collected toys for tots that year. We were able to obtain addresses for the needy in the area from the welfare department and could then deliver to them the gifts we had collected. That year was the first time we forgot our own children at Christmas. All of us, including the children, got totally involved in packing boxes with canned goods, dry goods and toys for the less fortunate. It became one of the greatest times of our lives. When I remembered it was Christmas and our children had nothing under the tree, I took forty dollars and went to the store to purchase Christmas presents for our four little ones.

When Frankie was twenty-one, he became associated with some very interesting people. He not only smoked pot; he was doing crack cocaine and prescription drugs, and also selling them. One night he went to Bel Air, Maryland, hoping to get prescription drugs from a drug store there. When the lady at the counter told him she couldn't sell him the medication he was asking for, he asked her if he could use the rest room. On the way up the hall to the rest room, he saw the lady's pocketbook, opened it and took her money.

She called me and asked if I had a son named Frank. I said, "Yes!"

She said, "He just robbed me. What should I do?"

I told her, "I have been praying for Frank for five years now, but God doesn't seem to hear me. Just call the police." She called Youth for Christ instead, and the next day a Pentecostal preacher called me. He told me who he was and asked if I had a son named Frank.

I said, "Yes, what has he done now?"

He said, "He hasn't done anything. I just want you to tell me about him."

When the conversation was over, the man prayed with me and sent ministering angels out and had them direct Frank to a telephone booth. His prayer was answered within thirty minutes. Frank called and asked how everything was? I told him to come home, that everything would be all right.

What an interesting way this was of finding the God we had been looking for all our lives. Frank came home, and the pastor came to speak with him. They met on the front porch, and the pastor was able to lead Frank to the Lord. But we were all impacted by his visit. Our life was never the same again.

The entire family went to church that Sunday, and we were all introduced to the Pentecostal faith: the lively music, the exuberant praise, the emphasis on the Word of God, the speaking in tongues, the prophecies and the healing miracles. I found it all to be "outstanding," but the rest of the family found it all to be "very strange," and they were reluctant to keep going.

Even though the rest of the family had pulled back, I continued to search for an understanding of these new teachings. In the process, the Lord drew me into His Word, and, for the first time in my life, I was able to understand it.

Suddenly the Bible seemed to be written just for me. I was so hungry to know Jesus that Dale bought me a set of audio tapes of the Bible, and we would listen to them at night after we had gone to bed.

I sought the Lord through radio and television ministries, through church and tent revivals, and any other way I could. As I changed, my life became a living witness, and Dale began to get curious about the change he saw in me. As we listened to the audio tapes together, the Lord began to draw him into His presence.

But Dale still didn't understand "this Pentecostal God" I had found, and he said he didn't believe that I was really changing. Instead, he became belligerent and critical, and I didn't know how to handle this attitude.

I went to the Lord and asked Him what to do about this. The thought that came to me in answer was this: *You submit to him and pray for him, and I will speak through him.* As I began to do this, the Lord began to heal my low self-esteem, and I began to like myself for the first time. As I submitted more and more to Dale, we stopped arguing about anything and everything. I found that I was no longer walking in unforgiveness, and that freed me to know who I was in Christ.

I discovered a small deliverance church in Joppa, Maryland. The pastor was from Trinidad, and so he understood the spiritual world. I had been in no other church with such understanding. It was there that the Lord began to give me the ability to understand the walk I had endured for so many years and the one I was now called to.

We, unfortunately, think the only world in existence is the one we can see with our physical eyes. I discovered that the true world I lived in was absolutely amazing. I discovered that God is a spirit, and so is the devil. When the devil was disobedient, Father God sent him to the earth to reside and chose to prove to him that He could have a people who would follow Him. Since Adam and Eve sinned in the garden and chose to walk in disobedience, they put the rest of creation into a place of decision.

God knew He would have to send His Son to the earth to take away the sins of the world, so He could have a people who would chose to follow Him and love Him. I am so glad I now learned to hear His voice and to follow His lead. In a very short time, life became so beautiful.

I know now that the only thing Father God expected from us was faith and obedience. With that, He is pleased with His children, and we are blessed abundantly.

Wow! I was learning some wonderful new and exciting things!

CHAPTER FOUR

THE BEGINNING OF MY CALL

The church at Joppa had a prayer group that got together every Saturday night, and Dale and I would attend. One night in that meeting, it was about 11:30 PM already, and Dale told me he wasn't getting anything to pray about, so he was going on home. I said, "Okay, but I can't leave yet." He told me to find a way home, and I did

After Dale left, the pastor asked if he could pray for my daughter. I said, "Yes." I went to stand in the circle and found myself on the floor in the middle of the group of people. No one had pushed me or even touched me. I heard someone screaming and discovered it was me.

Then I found myself being thrown about. When I came to myself and got up from the floor, I began to shake. The pastor said, "It isn't over yet," and he wrapped me in a blanket.

Then I began to have the dry heaves. I ran to the bathroom to vomit, and the last demon I passed was black. When it came out, another sister saw it. That black demon was witchcraft. I had witnessed many deliverances and didn't believe they were real ... until it happened to me. I felt like someone had taken a toothbrush and washed my brain. I had never had such clear thinking before (or since).

Dale and I began to gather with the youth of the church in an old barn that was behind the main building. They had a pool table on the first floor, but when you would go up the stairs to the second floor, we could put forty or fifty chairs up there around the walls. After the young people played and ate downstairs, they would filter up to the second floor and sit around the room. We were then able to share the Gospel with them. The group grew from a dozen to around forty in two months. Young people would come there all the way from Essex.

Then, one day the pastor told me his son was going to minister and, for some reason, I rebelled against that. These were our meetings. The result was that the group quickly disbanded. Through that I learned a hard lesson about rebellion and obeying those in authority. God blesses obedience and does not bless rebellion.

The Lord gave me a new friend named Patricia, and she later became my mentor, teaching me many things. Pat had a son named Mark, and Mark, who was bipolar, was very rebellious and could not get along with his step-father. It was this situation that led Mark to become the first of many young "guests" in our home. He bunked with Bill in the upstairs bedroom. With Mark in the house, we began to get more involved with deliverance ministries. We were able to take him to a deliverance service, and we worked with him at home to try to get him free.

We had purchased a house trailer with the idea of setting it up in our yard, but then, when we were not able to get permission from the county to do that, we kept it on the car lot in front of our property, and Dale and I took up residence there. At first, we just put a mattress on the floor, and that is where we slept.

One night, about 11 PM, I heard Billy's car start up. I got up to see what was happening, and the car pulled away from the house. I was left wondering where Bill was going at that time of the night.

At 2 AM, I got up again and discovered he still hadn't come home. I went to the house, only to find that it hadn't been Bill who left. It was Mark, and he had not only taken Bill's car; he had also taken his paycheck.

I called Patricia and told her what had happened. She immediately prayed and asked the Lord to send ministering angels out to block the car and to stop Mark from leaving the area. No one had any idea why he would have taken the car. We later learned that he had planned to go to New York. He had not gotten very far, however, only to Edgewood, Maryland, about fifteen miles away. The car had kept stalling on him, and he'd had to have it hot-wired three different times.

The police were called, and wouldn't you know it? What Pat had prayed was exactly what happened. A policeman spotted the car going behind the shopping center in Edgewood, and when he relayed this to another policeman, this one was on the other side of the shopping center. Together, they did exactly what Pat had asked for — they blocked Mark in.

The police called us and when we got there and discovered it was Bill's car, the policeman looked at Dale and said, "You are really lucky; you must know someone."

Dale looked up and said, "Yes, we do."

Little by little, the Lord was drawing Dale into His presence and revealing Himself to him in many unusual ways. This was the first of many wonderful experiences and the beginning of a whole new life.

Mark was locked up, and when he went to court, the judge asked Bill what he thought should happen to Mark. Dale and I had discovered Teen Challenge and had discussed this with Bill. So Bill now said to the judge, "If Mark is willing to go to rehab, I would like to see him recover." The result was that the judge released Mark into our custody, and we took him home ... intending to get him into the Teen Challenge Program in the Washington, DC Rehab Center.

To keep Mark from running again, we put another mattress on the floor of the trailer, and he slept there with us for the next three days. Then he went into the Teen Challenge program. Dale told him that if he would stay and complete the program, we would take him back. If, however, he "messed up," he should not call us. Mark refused to give up smoking and decided he really didn't want anyone to control his life, so he was in the facility for two days and then left. Sadly, he ended up in prison.

Patricia had a relationship with God that I wanted. She walked in a faith like no other person I had ever met. She and I decided we should can tomatoes for the winter, so we went out and purchased forty tomato plants, hoping to grow enough tomatoes, not only to can, but also to share with our friends and family. When the plants became mature, however, they became infected with a fungus.

One day when I went to the garden, I noticed all the tomatoes looked like white fuzz balls. When I shared with a Christian sister in the church about the plants having a fungus, the sister told me to go to The Home Depot and purchase a certain product, and by using that, we could get rid of the fungus. I did what she said, purchasing the product and mixing it in a bucket. When I went to put it on the plants, however, my sprayer broke, so I put the liquid back in the bucket, dipped it out and poured it on the plants. I then waited the required four days, but the plants still looked sick.

When Pat called and asked how our tomato plants were doing, I told her what I had done and the fact that they weren't doing very well. She said, "Anoint them with oil."

"That sounds crazy to me, " I said. "You come and anoint them."

Pat came over, and we went into the kitchen together to get the oil. When I took the bottle of oil out of the closet, it felt like I had stuck my hand into an electric socket. God was in it. We proceeded to anoint our hands and then danced and sang all through the rows of tomatoes. Within four days, there was not one blighted tomato plant in the garden. (Instead, the blight had moved back and infected the dead squash at the back of the garden). This was one of the most amazing things I had ever experienced.

That year we were able to give away many bushels of tomatoes, and we also canned tomatoes to use through the winter. Can't you just see the Father looking down and smiling? He has a great sense of humor, He uses the foolish things of this world to confound the minds of the wise (see 1 Corinthians 1:27). I am so glad that God sent Pat into my life.

Several weeks later, a lady came to my home and gave me a big box of Christian books. One of the books was about people's names, their meanings, and related scriptures. I found these things to be very inspiring. Because the Lord had revealed to me that I had a previously-hidden artistic talent, I was able to draw pictures that went with each meaning.

The Beginning of My Call

Someone taught me the technique called stippling, and I used that technique to start making greeting cards (computers had not yet been invented). This provided another opportunity for the Lord to teach me to know and understand His Word.

I would take a name, look up the meaning of it and then create a picture to go with that meaning by stippling. It was an arduous process, especially when I made a mistake and had to start all over again. But it was a great way to learn the Word, writing it over and over again.

Once I had developed enough cards to show and sell, I was able to set up a table at a school bazaar. One young man came to my table, and during our conversation, I began telling him about how my home had become a "holding tank" for young adults. He told me about his brother Willie who right then needed a place to stay. He gave me the telephone number where Willie worked, and I called him and invited him to meet with Dale and myself.

Dale decided to put Willie in a room in a motel up the road from us until he could check him out better. When he learned that Willie knew our boys, however, we invited him to come to stay with us, and he stayed for the next three years.

Willie brought a guitar with him and turned our home into a paradise of music. It was the most interesting and fulfilling time of my life. Good would come from it, but so would confusion and fear. Most importantly, we were learning obedience.

It always seems that when the Lord begins to work, the devil comes (with all his friends) and tries to stop the process. But what the devil means for harm God uses for good. For us, the only unfortunate thing that came out of this experience was that our daughter Donna later felt she had been cheated out of her childhood by all of this extra activity. The evil one blinded her and kept her from seeing the truth. But our attitude toward her never changed. We always loved Donna and always will.

Father God had been so good to us. How could we not reach out to others and extend the same goodness to them? But Donna was only fourteen when all of this began, and it seemed that the same anger I had felt for my mom was now being transferred to her. Donna was blinded to what the evil one was doing and how he was causing division in our home.

When God creates us, He puts a soul and spirit into a body. He gives us the ability to feel, and we become a person who learns how to live in the five senses. His objective was to create a people who would choose to love Him, but it is so hard when we walk by sight. God, therefore, sets out to put in our path many circumstances that will allow us to change our way of thinking and see His goodness.

It's just like the story of Adam and Eve. They looked at the tree, saw that the fruit was beautiful, tasted it and found it to be delicious, and then they were caught in the circle of confusion. The evil one is good at deception, but God is better at winning.

The hardest part is letting go so that God can do His work. Only Father God understands, from the beginning to the end. We walk in shortsightedness. Unless we choose to change our direction and choose to walk by the Spirit instead of by sight, we will continue to fall, and so will those around us whom we love so very much.

The next person who came to live in the home was a young lady. Only later did we learn that she was pregnant. I led her to the Lord, and she was not only saved but also baptized in the Holy Spirit. She truly fell in love with Jesus.

She first shared the news of her pregnancy with her boyfriend, thinking that he would accept the situation and marry her. He didn't. Instead, he told her he would take her back if she had an abortion. When I learned of this exchange, my response to her was, "No, you can't do that. You are a child of God, and that is murder."

She left our home and decided to have the abortion anyway. (The Lord was creating a situation for a big miracle to happen.) I went to the bedroom and screamed out to the Lord, and I heard a voice. The Voice said, "Darlene, I will stop it." I opened my eyes, thinking I would see my husband, but there was no one there.

When I saw that there was no one in the room with me, I decided it must be God who had spoken to me. After all, he had saved David when he was born, so why shouldn't I trust Him to save this baby as well? I wept for the next four days. I was believing God for a miracle, but I still couldn't get rid of the fear. This was another opportunity for the Lord to reveal His goodness and His arm extended.

On Thursday of that week, Patricia took me to a prayer meeting, and that night I received my prayer language. On Friday I found a piece of paper on the arm of my chair in the living room. I picked it up and began to read. It said "Hillcrest Heights Clinic" and there was a telephone number. I had no idea how that paper had come to be on the arm of that chair.

At 10 AM, I heard the same voice tell me to pray. I began praying in my new prayer language, and at 10:30, I heard the words "It is finished." I had no idea what that meant, but I felt I was about to find out.

The next day, as I looked out of my kitchen window, I saw the boyfriend going into Dale's garage. I went down and confronted him. I asked him where he had gone the day before. He said, "Why?"

I asked him if he had gone to Hillcrest Heights Clinic. He shook his head affirmatively. Then I asked him if they had gone in at 10 AM and found out they couldn't have the procedure done at 10:30 AM. Again he shook his head yes. Now his face turned white, and he couldn't speak.

I left the garage knowing that I had found the God I had been searching for since I was ten years old, and I was determined that no one would ever take Him from me. This was the greatest experience I had in finding the Lord. God never gives up on us, when He has chosen us to be anointed and sent out to draw other broken people into His presence.

But then I became very prideful, and the Lord had to humble me. He did this in His own way. Our son Bill had a love for wildlife, and one day, when returning from a trip to Florida, he got the idea of bringing home a small alligator. I asked him where he planned to keep it when it got bigger, and he said, "In the bathtub." Thank God the thing never grew up.

Bill had bought a fish aquarium, and he put the alligator in that. Later that day the Lord gave me a vision in which I saw the alligator lying on its back with its head under water. It had drowned. I went to Bill and told him that he should let some of the water out of the tank so that his alligator wouldn't drown. He said to me, "Mom, alligators don't drown."

That night, I got up three times to check on the alligator. The third time, sure enough, he was lying on his back. He had drowned. The next day I called our pastor and asked him to agree with me in prayer. "The Lord told me that just as Lazarus was raised from the dead after three days, Bill's alligator will come back to life."

Pastor thought this was a little "off the wall," and he was right. It wasn't the Lord who had told me that; it was my own prideful thoughts.

By the second day, the alligator became very stinky. I put him in a shoebox and set it out on the porch. When he didn't resurrect by the third day, I needed to understand why, so I began to read God's Word to find an answer. I knew it would be in there, for God is always faithful to give us an answer when we seek Him.

As I was turning to the book of Psalms to read, I happened to glance down at the last chapter of Job. There is spoke of Leviathan, and Leviathan was an alligator, so that got my attention. I called Patricia and told her what had happened, and she said to me, "Don't you know who Leviathan is? That is the name of the demon who is the chief of pride." The Lord used that alligator experience to deliver me from pride. I threw the alligator in the trash can, and the Lord began a new era in our lives that day.

Two men came to stay with us, one named Donald and another named David. Sometimes the Lord does some interesting things to bring about His perfect will. He used these two men and Willie in Dales's life to introduce him to the Word of God and teach him to come to know and love the Jesus whom I loved so very much.

Donald came to the church one night with his guitar to play music and discovered that Dale and I had an open house every Sunday after church, and many people would come by and fellowship. We met David at the church the same way. Both men came to stay with us. I had prayed and asked the Lord to reach Dale, because I couldn't, and this was the way He chose to do it.

These men would sit around at night for hours, discussing the Word of God. Donald was very knowledgeable about the Word and was on his own track to a miracle. He was believing that he and his wife would reconcile (and they eventually did). While he was waiting for his miracle, God sent him to us.

One night Dale, Willie, David and I went to a local convenience store to purchase some things, and there sat a girl on her luggage at a phone booth. When I went past her, the thought came to me that we should take her home with us. I went back to the car and told the men to pray. "The girl on the phone is going home with us."

They laughed, and one of them said, "That's not possible; she's high on drugs." Within twenty minutes the girl and her luggage were loaded in our car, and up the road we went. Her name was Donna, and she stayed with us for the next two months.

One day, as I was standing on our footbridge, I saw Donna coming down the road from a roadhouse that was up the street. I asked the Lord what to do and He instructed me to tell her, "We took you out of the world; now the world has to come out of you." She wasn't happy with that and proceeded to go in the house and pack her things.

She called a friend, and within an hour or two, she was gone. I didn't know what the Lord wanted to do in Donna's life; I just understood I needed to listen to His directions. Within two weeks, Donna called to tell us she had been raped and left for dead on the side of the road and to ask if she could come back. She wanted to know the Lord we had been telling her about. Donna came back to live with us and found the Lord, and her whole life was changed.

One day a young man named Salem accompanied by a young girl came across our parking lot and up to the front door and asked if they could use the phone. If I hadn't known better, I would have believed that there was a sign out in front of our property: ROOM FOR RENT. The young girl stayed only a short time, but Salem stayed with us for two years. He had multiple personalities and was bipolar.

We didn't force him to leave. He said that our home was the only place he had ever found peace. But he felt it was time to move on, and wanted to go home to Pennsylvania. Dale found him a car, and we were able to help him get insurance, and he went on his way.

If we are walking in obedience and following the Lord by faith, the devil is never allowed to come into our lives (unless the Lord has a purpose and desires to lift us up to a higher anointing). Satan can do nothing in our lives that the Lord doesn't allow, and if the Lord allows it, He purposes it. And if He purposes it, it is to bring glory to His Son Jesus.

We are God's vessels, and it is His choice how He uses us to attain to the fulfillment of His purpose. Willie, Donald and David began setting music up in our home in the evening, and we would all worship and praise together. It was so powerful that I could almost feel the walls shaking. Amazingly, people would come from all over.

A preacher from Essex called and asked Donald if we could come and sing at a carnival fundraiser he was having to fund a youth center. Donald was able to obtain a stage and five other groups to sing and play on it. In this way, we were able to bring Christian music to the carnival.

The preacher then asked if we would take care of the money booths. He believed he could keep more of the revenue if Christians took care of its collection. I had found a large rock near the booths, and I would sit on it each night, and the Lord would send people to sit with me. The time was never wasted. I met a lot of people who were hungry to know Jesus. Who would believe the Lord could use a carnival to introduce His Son to others? I learned God can use anything, anytime and anywhere He chooses. He is amazing!

One of the ladies who worked with us in the booths had a daughter who was about to go to prison, and that daughter would come and sit with each one of us on the nights we worked the booths. When she was eventually incarcerated in the Towson Detention Center, we were asked to go there and sing and minister to the girls. When we got there, the chaplain surprised us by asking if any of us would like to take over as chaplain of the women's section. I felt this was God's call for me, and so I accepted.

Isn't it amazing! The Lord takes a group of people to a carnival, and a lost girl comes and somehow God turns it all into a ministry. I became Chaplain of the women's prison and served in that capacity for the next twelve years.

Each time the Lord moved me to a new level in anointing, I learned to hear His voice more intensely. He taught me, not only to hear His voice, but also not to be afraid of anything. With my appointment as Chaplain, a new anointing came. The Lord began to use me in prophecy, and I saw many miracles happen in that prison. By the time I left that ministry, I had learned that we can do nothing without the anointing.

The last several years of that ministry, Dale began to accompany me and to share God's glory. The Lord not only blessed him by using him to minister, but He also humbled him. Dale was never able to minister there without weeping.

In that prison, the Lord was able to give me an understanding that could never be received anywhere else. We are all bound in one way or the other, and there are times when we find ourselves in a human prison of our own making. In that prison, I would see grandmoms, moms, and daughters together. I asked the Lord why this was, and He told me that the bondages had begun when the women were very young and were abused physically, sexually, or emotionally. Now they would have to be taught to break that vicious cycle. Because of their abuse, they would seek to be loved, and the only way they knew to love and be loved was physically.

A "John" would come along, use them, and then walk away, and instead of feeling better, the next day they would hate themselves even more. They would seek to hide from their disgust of themselves and often turn to drugs to be able to deal with their plight. In time, they would end up back in prison.

Those of us who are fortunate enough not to end up in prison, often deal with a harder prison. It is a prison of our soul. We stay bound because we don't recognize the plight we have put ourselves into. Therefore we walk in denial and continue to hide from the truth. We don't like anyone to point out our weaknesses, and we rebel against and generally push away those who are trying to help us. If only we would seek the humility to admit that we need help, we could find it. The Lord says that when we ask for wisdom, understanding, and knowledge, Father God is able and willing to give it to us in abundance (see James 1:5). What are we waiting for?

In Gods Spirit
A poem by Willie Wojeck

The Voice of One Broke

As I pick up my pen, I begin to write.
The Spirit leads like a hallway light.
It's never clear what I'm going to say,
But I trust that He'll move me in His way,
To give these words, to speak to you,
For all the love He's shown through you.
And it's a gift that's given, to be the one
Whom God has used to share His Son.
Through your loving heart and gentle ways
As you've given years, hours and days,
To take in the poor, the wretched, the broken,
To move in a way which God has spoken.
Though few, it seems, can understand a rem-
nant,
A thread, a scarlet strand,
Still more in the body, in spirit true,
This once-poor, wretched, broken man was
healed THROUGH YOU!

Chapter Five

Our Maturing Years

Dale had his first heart attack when he was fifty-seven, and this began a new chapter in our lives. I was only fifty-four at the time and was helping to raise two grandchildren, but now I decided that I had to go to work.

I found a job at the Fallston Hospital and discovered a new way to care for people. It was then that the Lord helped me to find four groups of people to take over the prison ministry. He showed me that I was now to minister to my husband and my grandchildren.

We were seldom able to follow the girls once they got out of the prison, but one day I asked the Lord to give me a prisoner who would become an overcomer and walk in victory after coming out. Several years later, I had a call from an African-American girl. She told me her name and asked me if I remembered her. I said I was sorry but I didn't. She then told me that she had been one of girls Dale and I ministered to in the Towson Detention Center.

She was also about to be one of two African American women to graduate from the Hebrew College in Pikesville, and she wanted to know if I would like to come to her graduation. What a blessing that was! She was my answer to prayer. This lady and I became close friends.

When the young people stopped coming to our home, we were taken down another path. We decided to move in with Dale's mom. She had become bedridden and needed full-time care. We were thinking of remodeling her basement and living in it.

But our son and daughter-in-law were having difficulties about then, and they asked if Dale and I would assume the responsibility of their girls. I knew we couldn't put those girls in my mother-in-law's basement, so I prayed about what we should do. Since my mother-in-law had a piece of property next door, I asked her if she would give it to us to build a house on. She not only gave us the property; she also gave us $60,000, so that we were able to build a house and furnish it.

One day I remember standing on her back porch, watching Dale as he worked with the sub-contractors, when the Lord suddenly spoke to me. He said, *"Do not be deceived: God cannot be mocked. A man reaps what he sows,"* Galatians 6:7). Father God always repays obedience. We not only had a new house, but we were able to put an apartment in the basement for our daughter and her two babies.

It was then the Lord began to reveal the answer to that promise He had spoken to me so many years before. Our property on Bel Air Road was sold in three parcels for $200,000, exactly what He had shown me long before.

A man who owned a business next door to us wanted to obtain fifteen feet of our frontage on Bel Air, and he offered us $15,000 and the ground between our property and the power line. This piece was also fifteen feet wide, and it extended the entire length of the property. We agreed to his offer and sold him the frontage.

Several months later a man on the other side of us requested that we sell him an acre of our land on the back side of the creek. He wanted to put a plumbing warehouse there, and he paid us $35,000. How did this all happen when the land had been declared unsalable?

One day I was standing in the office, and I saw three well-dressed men coming down the road and across our property. I told Dale to go out and see what they wanted. They went up on the footbridge, and it was obvious that they were discussing the property.

These were representatives of the county, and when they saw how the creek was undermining the house, they decided, after much discussion, to fix it. To do this, they cleaned out a stone quarry and used the scrap stones to bank the creek. It was a major project because it had to be done on four hundred feet of the stream.

When this was all finished, it resolved the flooding problem we had been suffering for years, and Dale was then able to rent the property for a used car business. That business proved to be very successful and, after about a year, the man who had rented the property decided that he would like to purchase both the business property and the house, and he did so — for $150.000. We held the mortgage for him for eleven years at 8% interest. This was the same property we had purchased for $25,000, the same property that had been condemned, and the same property the Lord had told me would sell for $200,000.

Now we took a whole new direction in life in our new home on Wilgis Road. We became foster parents to the whole neighborhood and lived there for nearly five years.

When my mother-in-law died, she left us very comfortable. Dale had lived ten years after that first heart attack, and now we decided to sell the house on Wilgis Road and invest in a house in Cecil County.

We found a piece of property in Conowingo. (It was there we raised Sarah and Christina, two of our grandchildren.) The owners were asking $167,000 for it, but Dale offered them $140,000.

One evening Dale and I went to a diner there in Cecil County and sat down at a table next to a group of people we didn't know. They were talking about a piece of property they had for sale and someone named

Graves had put a bid on it for $140,000. That caught our attention.

They decided to take the offer and really surprised us. They had no idea that the people that had given them the offer was sitting at the table next to them. Needless to say we were shocked and also blessed.

The property we purchased for $140,000 had three pieces of property with it and was located on Bel Air Road in Conowingo. One piece had a main house with three bedrooms. The second piece had a large dog kennel on it, which we were able to turn into a three-bedroom home, to rent to our daughter and her husband and children. And the third piece was just an empty lot.

Because the middle piece had a previous building on it, we were able to obtain a building permit to build the extra house. Then Donna's husband Mike got a piece of cement in his eye and couldn't work for a year. Since he was a builder, he was able to build the three-bedroom house for us. Then they rented it from us for $150 a month. God is so good. He knows the beginning from the end, and He never fails us—if we only trust and believe. They rented from us until Donna and Mike split up.

Dale, Sarah, Christina and I continued to live in the main house, and Frank, the girls' father, came to stay with us often. Frank was addicted to cocaine, and this was the beginning of me attending meetings concerning addiction. He really wanted to get free. One day, after Frank had used the washer, I was washing clothes, and when I pulled my clothes out of the washing machine, I found a bag of white powder mixed in with them. I said, "Oh, wow! Dale, look at this! What do you think this is?"

He said, "I don't know, but I intend to find out."

When Frank came home that evening, Dale held up the bag and asked him, "What is this?"

"Give it to me," Frank said. "It's worth $100."

After praying about it, Dale decided to ask Frank to leave. For too long we had both been enablers. Frank wanted to get free from drugs, but didn't know how, and we didn't know how to help him.

As I noted earlier, because of our codependency, Dale and I were the worst thing that happened to our children. But we walked in denial and didn't understand our part in their addiction. It was because of this addiction that we had the responsibility of raising our granddaughters. When she was eleven, Christina decided to leave and move back with her mom, but Sarah stayed with us till she was eighteen.

On December 14, 2001, at the age of sixty-seven, Dale died. I was just sixty-four. We had lived happily in Conowingo for eleven years. Suddenly, life took a serious turn. I had never had to make important decisions in my whole life. When I was still at home, Dad had made them, and once I was married to Dale, he had made them. I now had to depend on a God I couldn't see and didn't know as much about as was needed.

At first it was very difficult, letting go of my own thinking and learning how to listen for that still, small voice that would direct me and not let me fall. Otherwise, I was all alone.

David and his wife Renee had a lot of dysfunction in their home, and on Christmas Day, just eleven days after Dale died, I sat and tried to reconcile them, but it didn't go well.

That next year, one of our granddaughters left her husband, and he came to live with me. His hope was that I could reconcile the two of them. I created scripture notes and put them all over the house, trying to create positive thoughts for his life. It was the only way I knew to give him hope. It didn't work. Prayer was needed, and I, unfortunately, wasn't able to pray warfare prayers as yet.

My life was so filled with depression that I just wanted to run away. After all, that was what I had learned to do as a little girl. Running away was my way of coping with anything unpleasant.

Toward the end of 2002, David was rushed to the hospital with what he and Renee thought was a ruptured appendix. Renee called me and asked me to come to the hospital. On the way to the hospital, the Lord spoke to me and said, "David will live." I couldn't imagine where that thought was coming from. After all I had been told he only had appendicitis.

Then I heard the same thing again. The second time the Lord said, "Remember the vision."

Then I realized it wasn't just a thought; it was the Lord.

When David had been sixteen, I had been in a time of prayer and had a vision of him being resurrected from the dead and getting up out of a coffin. Now I didn't know what to think. I just continued to sing and praise the Lord, as I drove toward the hospital.

When I got there, David had been in surgery for over an hour. Renee and I decided to go out and get some lunch. When we came back, some four hours later, a doctor came into David's room. He had a nurse with him, and he immediately closed the door and turned off the TV. Having worked in a hospital for many years, I knew this wasn't a good sign. He proceeded to tell us that David was in recovery, but there had been a tumor in his stomach, it had burst, and he didn't know for sure whether David would make it or not.

I said, "Oh, no! David will live!"

"I can't tell you that," the doctor replied.

"But my Father God told me he would live, as I was on the way up here, and He doesn't lie," I said.

"Well, I can't argue with that," the doctor humbly responded.

And David did live, but he had to undergo radium treatments for the next six months. Then he had another tumor removed. Later he had to go back for a third surgery, this time to insert netting into his abdomen to hold his organs in place. I can say that David is now fifty-three years old, and he still lives.

The year 2003 was one with many challenges for me. In January of that year I fell on the ice and broke two disks in my spine and a rib. My grandchildren took me to the hospital. I was sent to a bone specialist.

The bone doctor said he was going to have to put me into a brace and then, after twelve weeks, he would have to give me special therapy. When I left the doctor's office that day the Lord spoke to me: "You praise me, and I will heal you."

The brace the doctor put on me covered my chest and held my shoulders in place. It was very big, very bulky and very cumbersome. When anyone would ask me what had happened to me, I would tell them how I had fallen, but then I would add that the brace was my breastplate of righteousness and that God was healing me. I was determined to praise Him through it all, and I really didn't care what anyone else thought about it. I was going to trust my Savior and Healer.

When I went back to the doctor for another x-ray, he was surprised and said, "There is no sign that you ever had anything broken." Well, that was a great miracle, but the greatest miracle of all was that I had long suffered from osteoporosis. Normally, it should have taken my bones a very long time to heal, if they healed at all. I have found that Jesus is the best Husband, Provider, Confidant, Director and so much more. He is far more capable than any of us give Him credit for. There is an old saying: *God helps those who help themselves.* But that's just not true. The truth is that God helps those who trust Him and learn to praise Him.

Problems are never easy to face, but life takes on a new perspective when you can look into the face of a problem and see the arm of the Lord extended. Take His hand and let Him lead you through the challenges of life. How would we ever get to know Him without some situation that we needed Him to fix? How would we ever have a testimony of His goodness if we never had anything to overcome and, therefore, could not learn how to be an overcomer? When you see life in this context, you quickly realize that problems are our friends, for they draw us closer to God.

That same year, just after David began to recover enough to go back to work, Renee asked him to leave. She said she had only been waiting for him to get better to tell him. She had a boyfriend she wanted to bring into the house.

David called me to say that Renee didn't want him anymore, and I went and picked him up.

The worst part of this breakup was the effect it had on their twelve-year-old son Christopher. Christopher became very bitter and resentful. Just as I had experienced in my childhood, the unwise actions of parents fall upon the innocent. Christopher now had to pay a dear price for his mom's selfishness, his dads insecurities and my ignorance.

Because I was still walking in grief over the loss of my beloved Dale (which I continued to walk in for eleven years), I wasn't including God in my thinking. So many Christians become born again and think that is the ultimate answer. The sad truth, however, is that they don't include God in their daily decisions. It is only because I have come down this road that I am now able to see and understand.

The Lord has shown me, through Revelation 12, that we will be free *"by the blood of the Lamb and by the word of [our] testimony"* (Revelation 12:11). Jesus had to die on the cross, but we need to realize that our cross is His. Because He paid the price, we need to trust and believe. When we don't, then we have to learn the hard way. Because we have lived through something, many times it gives us understanding that only God can give. I packed David and his clothes into my car and moved him into my home.

Soon, however, David began having hallucinations, and I spent the next two years trying to deal with his addictions. I kept trying to send him away, but he wouldn't stay gone. My life was so overwhelming that I wasn't able to take care of the property, and the mortgage and taxes and so on and so on. I began to be concerned about the upkeep of the house. It was overwhelming and just more than I could emotionally deal with.

I asked Donna to buy the house she was living in with Fred and offered it to them for $130,000. I thought maybe if I paid off the property I would be able to handle the other expenses. But I didn't pray and ask God what to do, which is what I should have done. Instead, I reasoned in my own mind.

The problem with that is we don't see the beginning from the end, so we play the what-ifs. Only Father God knows what the ending will be.

When Donna said "no," she didn't want to pay that much for the house, I decided that we all had to move. I sold the property God had blessed us with, and this enabled me to become financially sound. In 2004, I saw a trailer park I liked in Elkton. I went to the sales office, picked out a new trailer and made it just the way I wanted it to be for the home of my retirement.

This also proved to be a mistake. Or did it? What the devil means for harm, God can turn around and bring good out of it. Yes, we make mistakes, but if our heart is right, and we are able to admit to those mistakes, Father God is able to turn things around for us. I believe everything in life is a learning experience. Our Father takes every one of our negative experiences and turns them into a positive. That is ... those we are willing to give to Him.

My new mobile home had four bedrooms, three baths, a porch on the back that I had glassed in and a porch on the front that I had screened in. Before I even moved in, someone broke in and stole my stove and dishwasher. I went to check the place out and found police tape around it. I was only able to get into it through a whole the thieves had made in the wall. The trailer park owner took responsibility for the loss and was able to get back the stove and dishwasher and to fix the hole in the wall, but my new life was not starting very well.

I was able to purchase new furniture, and I had started my new life ... or so I thought. Because we are created to live in the flesh and until we are able to grab hold of the hand of the Lord, we are always trying to do His work for Him. I didn't realize that is what an enabler does. I didn't even realize yet that I *was* an enabler.

David and I now moved to Elkton, and Linda, a friend of mine, also came to live with us. The fourth bedroom I turned into an office. Linda was with us just a year and then decided to move.

One Sunday, as I was sitting in the front row of a church in Elkton, I heard the Lord speak to me and tell me to turn to Hebrews 5. I began to read, and when I got to verse 8, I read this:

Son though he was, he learned obedience from what he suffered.

I sat back and asked, "Why did He have to suffer? He was God."

Then the Lord said to me, "I gave My Son for you, but you won't give me yours."

I sat there and wept. It was 2005 when He spoke this to my heart, but I wasn't able to give David up until 2009.

I didn't want to wait and see. I wanted an instant change. But, again, I wasn't aware that I was serving David as an enabler. Most enablers aren't aware of it. I didn't even know what denial was, until the Lord was able to get my attention.

After David moved with me, he began hanging out with and bringing home the wrong kinds of people. Enablers are always trying to do God's work for Him. When would I ever learn?

Chapter Six

Overcoming Complications

When we are caught in our own misery, we become very selfish. Consequently, our lives become very dysfunctional. David began using more and more drugs, and I also began turning into a dysfunctional mess. One day I went to open my safe and found it emptied. I had been gathering coins, and I asked David if he knew where they were. Of course he said no. "Someone must have broken into your safe," he said, "I don't know anything about it."

I went into his bedroom to make the bed and found a receipt lying on the back headboard shelving. It was from a pawn shop. I took the receipt and went to the pawn shop, explaining to the man that my son had stolen my coins. Amazingly, he gave them back to me.

I still couldn't bring myself to put David out. He was the son the Lord had saved as a baby, The Lord had kept him at twenty-two from becoming paralyzed when he lifted heavy pipes and his two lower discs had burst and were severing his spinal column, and

He had saved him again at forty-one when he had cancer and was not given any chance at all to survive. Then his wife had put him out. How could I let him go?

One day he called me and said he needed a ride. I went and picked him up and brought him home. I dropped him off, and then I went on to work.

I was troubled because on the way back to the house, David had told me he didn't want to live anymore. This caused me a lot of fear, and I called Donna and asked her what she thought I should do. She went to the Court House and filled out paperwork to have her brother committed to the hospital.

When Donna and I got to the house, David told us the police had come and asked if there was anyone there who was suicidal. As he began to tell us about this, I became very nervous and sat and shook. Donna began having serious words with David.

While this was going on, Fred, Donna's boyfriend, stayed outside, watching through the screen door. When the police came again, they came up behind him and asked what he was doing there. He told them he was just watching what was going on inside the house.

David was becoming very angry with us, so the police came in and dealt with the situation. As I look back on it now, it was like a scene out of a movie. David agreed to go to the hospital, but only if I would take him. I told the policemen that I wasn't afraid of him; I was only afraid *for* him. He ended up in the psyche ward and then I began outpatient therapy. I was about to have a nervous breakdown myself.

Billy and Donna decided that I needed to live with one of them. Bill had no room, so Donna decided to find a house that could accommodate us all, and she found one in Conowingo. I sold my beautiful trailer and moved into a mother-in-law suit in the basement of the new house.

I received $120,000 for the trailer. $65,000 of that was in cash, and I held the mortgage for the rest, which gave me about $500 a month income for the next four years. I gave Donna the $65,000 as my investment toward the purchase the new home and the creation of the mother-in-law suit.

It was agreed that I would live there for the rest of my life — provided David would not come there, even for a visit. Then one night he showed up at the door. He had been pistol-whipped, so I allowed him to spend the night on my sofa.

The next morning I woke at 4 AM and started to get ready to take a grandson to court. When I went into the bathroom, I slipped on the tile floor, fell on the toilet seat and broke my ribs. David heard the commotion, came into the bathroom and found me on the floor.

I asked him not to touch me, just to leave me there and call for help, but he had other ideas. He brought a chair, picked me up from the floor, and sat me on the chair.

I stopped breathing, and when I came to, I saw that the room was full of my grandchildren. Then I saw the ambulance crew coming in the door. I remember hearing someone calling my name at a far distance. I had told them to just leave me alone. It was so peaceful where I was that I didn't want to be bothered. But that person wouldn't stop calling me.

I had stopped breathing, had wet myself and had turned blue. In short, I died! When I came to, I asked David why the floor was all wet, and he told me what had happened. I was placed in the ambulance and was taken to the hospital. Thank God, David had come home that night. I guess God had more for me to do. I was healed, and David and I moved. I purchased a small trailer in Pennsylvania and began another new venture in my life. This was the third move I had made since Dale died.

The thought that I needed to release David for his own good never left me. One day, in 2009, I was out on the front porch, and I looked up to God and said, "Father, he's Yours. Where would you have me go?"

The Father said, "I want you in Maryland."

I didn't hear anything else, so I began to think and pray about where He wanted me to go. First I considered that maybe He wanted me to take the trailer to Conowingo and put it in the yard behind the house. I called my sister Leslie and told her what I was thinking about, and she asked me to come live with her.

Overcoming Complications

In the end, I decided that I couldn't live with my sister; we were both too headstrong, and it just wouldn't work. Instead, I decided to move to Waldorf, Maryland.

I went to visit Leslie, and when I got back home, I found holes in the walls where someone had hit them. I wept. I went to work that day, and when I came home, David was already in bed. He said, "Hi, Mom, how are you?"

I said, "Not so good. I am moving." And then I added, "And, after you fix the walls, you are too."

David said, "Okay, I understand." And he left.

I began to make the arrangements for this move. I had to quit my job, sell my home, and arrange to move my furniture. Father would do the rest.

I gave notice to the hospital and told my boss I would be leaving in August. Then, suddenly, my foot began to give me a problem. Several years before this I had gone to a foot doctor, and he had told me I had an extra bone in my foot. He said he would have to put a screw in the foot to hold the cartilage in place. Now the screw was backing out of my foot, I couldn't walk, and it gave me a lot of pain.

Father gave me grace to know what to do. I had to go back to my boss and tell her about the situation and that I wouldn't be able to work for her for the time I had promised. She agreed to let me stay on the payroll so that I could get the surgery I needed.

When my foot was examined more thoroughly, it became clear that I didn't really have an extra bone in my foot at all, and I hadn't really needed a screw in my foot to hold the cartilage in place. The pain I was suffering was due to a fall I had suffered some years before. A piece of bone had broken off and had now worked its way to the surface, and it just needed to be removed. The Lord was using my circumstances again to give me grace for this move. He had some things to work out.

As we look at our situations and we begin to fear, we just can't see the whole picture. When we begin to fear, we begin to run ahead and try to fix whatever is broken. If we could just wait and trust and begin to praise God for His resolution to the situation, He would do the work. For He is very able to make everything right.

I arranged to have my foot operated on, and Bill picked me up from the hospital. As we were leaving the hospital, my cell phone rang. It was Ed in Elkton, the man I had sold the mobile home to and was holding the mortgage for. He asked me if I could stop by; he had a check for me.

When we got to Elkton, Ed told me that his retirement check had come and he wanted to pay off the balance of the mortgage on the mobile home. He gave me a check for $20 more than I had needed to buy the trailer in Conowingo. God is good.

I was co-owner of the house that Donna had purchased, having $65,000 invested in it, but now I decided that $65,000 was a small price to pay to be reconciled to her. I let her keep it.

My sister Pam had a spa in Waldorf, and Leslie was her office manager. I went there to get my hair done. The lady in the office across the hall from Leslie gave her resignation, and I was given a job.

Just up the road from the trailer park where I settled on Cedarville Road was a Pentecostal church, and it was there the Lord wanted me to go now. God used the new pastor of that church to direct me to Celebrate Recovery. He had come there just six weeks after I began attending. The Lord had to send me one hundred miles away from my family to free me from codependency.

I had no idea that I needed to be free, I honestly thought that I had it all together. But when I found the Celebrate Recovery that I chose to attend, I began to discover who I really was.

It took two years to free me. The first year I attended the meeting, and the second year I helped facilitate a meeting. The third year I became involved with a lady who had Alzheimer's, and I wasn't able to help her. The frustration was horrible.

Then I began attending a group meeting for the Stephens Ministry. It was a fifty-week course, and this one began in January 2012. I thought I was going to work with prisoners coming out of prison, but the Lord had a different idea. I got viral pneumonia in January 2013, lost fifteen pounds in five days and decided I really didn't want to live alone any longer. I prayed and reminded the Lord of what He had said in His

Word, that He takes the single person (the lonely or solitary) and puts them in a family (see Psalm 68:6). Three weeks later my granddaughter called me and told me she had been thinking for the last two weeks she should ask me to come and live with her. What a blessing! I put my trailer up for sale that February, sold it in March, and moved in with her in April.

Only God knows what we need. Just when I thought life was over, it had just begun. I have met so many new people and have been used to free some. Some won't listen, but if I allow Him to, He knows just where to put me and what I should be doing for His glory.

The Lord has taught me to love Him with all my heart and to love others as I love myself. The secret is to learn to love yourself first. You can't help another person if you don't allow the Lord to first pull you out of the pit. I am still learning to know and understand who I am, through the experiences that I suffer.

As long as we live on this earth, we never stop learning. Father uses the experiences we encounter to give us a testimony, so we can help others. It is an exciting way to live, knowing there is Someone greater than me to lead me and guide me, and that person doesn't have to be a human. This takes all the fear out of the things I do, the places I go, and the people I come in contact with. As long as I seek the wisdom of the Lord, I will never fail. In every situation I will either be blessed or taught. It is up to me to receive and to put into practice the things I learn.

Overcoming Complications

Each one of us has our own road to travel. That's what makes life so exciting. My prayer for anyone who reads this is that God will bless you and keep you, and may His light shine upon you and May you walk in His grace and mercy.

Chapter Seven

Looking Back

I'm seventy-eight now, and as I look back I can see the hand of God on my life. Father God never does anything in vain. We are the ones who, all too often, set aside His goodness and gifts. If we would live by the two commandments Jesus gave us – *"Love the Lord your God with all your heart and with all your soul and with all your mind"* and *"Love [others] your neighbor as yourself"* (Matthew 22:37-39) — there is nothing we are incapable of doing. He taught me to trust Him by realizing that whatever experience is given to me, He will make it perfect. All I have to do is demonstrate faith in Him. Hebrews 11:1 shows that we cannot please Him without it.

After my deliverance, I began to understand His call on my life, and I choose to walk in obedience. Hebrews 5:8 says that Jesus walked in obedience, and that is why He could be the only one to sit on the right hand of God interceding for us day and night. I came to realize that I will never become perfect; I will always walk in my feelings; but it's what I do with them that decides whether I am victorious or whether I lose the battle. Until I go home to be with the Lord, I will always be tested by the evil one, because our battle is not against flesh and blood, but against powers and principalities of darkness. I have also learned that I can't out-give God.

I have four living children, ten grandchildren and five great-grandchildren. Because of my codependency, the Lord first took the love of my life. Then He separated me from all my children by opening the door for me to move a hundred miles away from them. He wanted to teach me about myself.

As I noted earlier, David followed me, and I allowed him to stay. But when he, too, was finally removed from my life, the stage was set. I had to come to the place of being bold enough to let go of everyone I loved. It wasn't an easy way to live, but, looking back now, I wouldn't trade my life for anything.

My Father in Heaven has become the best Husband I could ever know. He allowed me to become very wealthy and then to lose it all and become homeless, but He has always come through to show me His love. With everything that has happened, I have never been hungry or without a place to lay my head. In this way, I have become a living witness to my children, grandchildren and great-grandchildren. What a blessing it is to know that my life speaks louder than words.

My children are scattered to the north, south, east, and west of me, but we still stay in contact, and they are much closer to me now than they were when we all lived together in the same house. And my whole life has been about seeking to be a blessing to the broken.

My first ministry was given to me when I had both feet operated on and had to spend time recovering. Dale asked what I would like him to do for me. I asked him to buy me some paints, and I set out to paint. Elvis Presley had just died, and I found a picture of him in a magazine and decided to paint his picture. Then I painted a picture of my dad. These were both very life-like. I could almost talk to Dad — even though he had been dead for many years.

I then found an ad in the newspaper that read: "If you have artistic talent, call us. We have a job for you." I called and was hired to retouch the negatives of high school and college students. As I did this, the Lord gave me the gift of discernment, and I began praying for each of those young people, hundreds of them in all. I might never know them, but God did.

As I prayed, I began to see in my mind's eye their struggle with drugs, alcohol, and other things — whatever the Lord wanted me to pray for. I wept for those young people as I did my job for the next two years. It was an amazing experience.

Then the church I was attending began a ministry of helps and that became my next responsibility. It was during the next three and a half years that we had young people coming to live in our home. In all, we had thirty-five young people come to stay with us during that time. We treated them as our own and did our best to win them to the Lord and help them with their struggles. Every evening we all worshiped and praised God together. Some of them were more of a blessing to us than we ever were to them.

Thinking back on that period, I believe that the three greatest gifts the Lord gave me were these: He taught me to love unconditionally, He helped me to forgive my mom (who had been dead for sixteen years), and He gave me a faith that moves mountains. He also used that time to save Dale's soul and to draw us both into a place of great peace.

Together with the young people who came to live with us, we then began a youth ministry in our church. We sang and testified on the street corners in Baltimore. It was during this time that the preacher from Essex met us and asked if we would come sing at the carnival he was having to raise money for the youth in his church.

As I noted earlier, one of the ladies who came to the carnival and helped run the money booths brought her daughter with her. The daughter had been found guilty of burning a barn with expensive horses in it, and she was soon to be locked up in the Towson Detention Center. That led to us being asked to go there and sing for the prisoners. Then the chaplain asked if any of us would like to volunteer to become chaplain over the women of the prison, and I said yes.

As I noted earlier, I ministered in the prison for twelve years, and Dale went with me the last six years. Once, as we were ministering, an argument took place between two inmates, and some girls at the back of the room began to rumble. I looked up to Jesus and asked, "What should we do?"

The Lord answered, "Drop to your knees and praise Me." I did that. The rumble stopped, and the girls began to cry and hug each other. They left the room that day different from when they had come in.

Another day, the girls began singing and praising God so loudly that five guards came rushing in, thinking that we were having a riot. When they saw what was happening, they backed respectfully out of the room and closed the doors.

When I left that day, the captain asked what she could do for me. I said, "Could you give me an extra thirty minutes."

She said, "You've got it." And that was a blessing from then on.

One day one of the girls asked me to pray for her. She was going to court the next day. I prayed, and then I told her she was going home. I went to court with her the next day, and the judge released her into my care.

When we got home, I took her to a church nearby and they gave me enough money to buy her a train ticket home and some clothes she could wear. That girl became a believer.

One day one of my granddaughters whom we were raising became frightened about the people we were taking in. I told her God would not send anyone to us who would hurt her. I truly believe my life is His to use, and He will do nothing to harm us.

So, that's my life until now. I can't wait to see what tomorrow holds.

Chapter Eight

God's Incomparable Love

When we are codependent, we cannot see the truth. We think we are walking in love, but we are really keeping those around us bound. It took me a long time to be set free from this. If we could only learn from someone else's mistakes, we wouldn't have to make as many of our own.

Our Lord is Love and, according to First Corinthians 13, we are to walk as He is. In closing this book, there is a beautiful passage in the *How to Find God New Testament* [1] that I would like to quote:

- God says love should be directed toward others (1 Corinthians 13:1-3). The world says love should be directed toward ourselves.
- God says love is patient and kind (verse 4).

---

1. *Holy Bible, New Living Translation*, copyright © 1996, 2004, 2007, 1013 by Tyndale House Foundation, Carol Stream, Illinois, page 206.

The world says love satisfies your immediate needs.

· God says love is never jealous or envious (verse 4). The world says love means that you deserve the "best."

· God says love is never boastful or proud (verse 4). The world says love isn't necessary to make people respect you.

· God says love is never rude (verse 5). The world says love lets you act as you please.

· God says love does not demand its own way (verse 5). The world says love gets in the way of what's in it for me.

· God says love is not irritable or touchy, and it holds no grudges (verse 5). The world says love takes a backseat when it comes to seeking revenge.

· God says love rejoices in justice and truth (verse 6). The world says love understands—even ignores—evil.

· God says love is loyal (verse 7). The world says love should be self-serving.

"The kind of love God wants us to give others is impossible to 'manufacture' on our own. You might say that it is a 'supernatural' love." It is a natural outflow of God's presence in our lives. That is why the Bible says, *'[God] has given us the Holy Spirit to fill our hearts with his love.'* "

I love this wonderful book, *How to Find God New Testament*. I buy them by the case and give them to anyone I meet who seems to be in need of a touch of God's love. This is another of my current ministries to others.

A Word from Willie Wojcik

My name is Willie Wojcik. I'm a believer in Jesus Christ, and my life has been paid for by His blood. The purpose of this writing is to bring to remembrance *"the wonderful works of God,"* as He has called us to do. These are my memories of Darlene Graves, whom I personally adopted as "Mom," for the reasons you will soon see.

Darlene was the second miracle to come to my life. The first was my salvation, when I accepted Jesus Christ into my heart. This happened shortly before I met her. I don't want to take up too much space talking about myself, but I must back up enough to explain how much of a miracle this all actually was for me.

I grew up as an abused child in Harford County, Maryland. I had a drunken, wife-beating, mentally- and physically-abusive father who helped hurl me into an out-of-control lifestyle. Because I was born in 1962, by the time I was thirteen (in 1975) that type of lifestyle was fairly common. Mine was a life of drugs, sex and eventually crime.

My father and I fought so much that I was sure to end up behind bars if I stayed at home. So, at thirteen,

I just left. My entire family is still in denial about that phase of my life to this day, but by the time I was eight I was already smoking marijuana. By the time I was nineteen, I had already done 500 trips on LSD, massive amounts of PCP, mushrooms and heart-stopping combinations of other chemicals. Although alcohol is as seductive as heroine, I never favored it for sheer hatred of my father.

Because of becoming so involved with drugs at an early age, I didn't have many relationships with girls. I tended to frighten them away. I didn't know how to love anyone because I had never known what real love was like. My mother had been too busy dodging Dad's fists to show me any affection, plus she had five other children to worry about.

After leaving home, I lived wherever I could. Sometimes that was in the woods. Sometimes I would stay in old abandoned houses or the tree houses of friends. God bless them.

Little by little, I started getting into trouble, mostly for the need of money, not only to exist, but also to support my drug habit. I robbed from drug dealers and local street cons. Some of the boys I hung with had serious underworld connections, and I quickly found myself being wanted by several unsavory groups.

As I grew toward manhood I messed with a couple of girls, and then I ended up with the wife of a business partner (so to speak), while he was in jail, and she led me into the Occult. I had already dabbled in it a little, using drugs for enchantments and perverting one of my first God-given abilities into something evil. As a child of five, I had shown promise in drawing and painting, but now I turned that talent into mind reading for profit. Somehow I was able to draw the things I saw in other people's minds just by speaking with them. I never tried to explain away the truth of Jesus, but I willingly chose to walk in darkness. My heart was turning ever more evil.

I made several suicide attempts, but my tolerance for chemicals was just too high to die that way. Then one night I slashed the tendons of my right arm. My brother-in-law intervened and got me a job in construction. He was also my guitar teacher. I liked playing, and within a short time, I started playing professionally in an original group (which, in the 1970s was not well accepted locally). If you weren't top 40 club music, you had to play the underground clubs, like the Marble Bar and the 9:30.

In the years that followed, I played on the same stage as some famous people—like Iggy Pop and Joan Jet—but I was so far gone on drugs that I didn't remember even being there. Thirty years later, someone else had to tell me about it. And no wonder I couldn't remember. I was crawling out of the bushes behind someone's house, being carried into a car and then getting on stage to play. I didn't know how I had gotten there or where I went when it was over.

This exaggerated use of drugs began to take its toll on my health. I was 6 foot 1 and 1/2 inches tall, but now I weighed only about 126 pounds wet.

I had to drop out of school because the police were looking for me, and the sad thing was that I could get A's in my classes and loved school. I was just too crazy for it.

When I had drained all of my relationships for drugs and was tired of living in the woods, I would sneak into the out-patient psych ward at a local hospital to bathe and steal food from the nurse's station. There was a boiler room in an old rundown motel where I sometimes slept on linen racks when it got really cold outside. I was homeless during the blizzard of 1979.

Then, one day, while I was at a rehearsal for an upcoming show, my younger brother called the house where we were practicing and asked if I would like to go with him to see a movie called *A Distant Thunder*. It was showing in an old church, he said. I didn't know he had been saved or what that even meant. I went, and it was there that God spoke to me through the words of a song entitled "I Wish We'd All Been Ready" by Larry Norman.

There's no time to change your mind.
How could you have been so blind?
The Father spoke, the demons dined.
The Son has come, and you've been left behind.

A Word from Willie Wojcik

I knew that I was on my way out. I would either overdose or be killed some other way soon, and eternity would not be a good experience for me. I wasn't on my way to a better place. That day I surrendered and received Jesus as my Savior.

But that was just the beginning of this story, not the end. My younger brother, who had taken me to that Church said, "I know God changed his heart, and Jesus is his Lord now, but what's going to happen to him? He's so burned out he can't even think anymore." And he was right.

Now that I was a true believer in Jesus, I had to somehow change the things in my life that were against my Lord. One-by-one He began to speak to me about lying and con games, etc. Marijuana and other drugs were part of the occult and witchcraft to me, and they had to go. I just needed His help to overcome them.

Weed was the first thing to go. I was miserable now trying to get high, and I gave it up that September, less than a month after of my conversion. Because I was losing my street con to Jesus and could no longer steal drugs or money to buy them, I also lost the ability to get an occasional night off the streets. I didn't have the trust of nice folks, and the old boys didn't want me around anymore. When people ask you why you don't smoke weed anymore, and you tell them that Jesus changed your life, either they quickly get tired of having you around, or they, too, get converted.

With no job, still physically frail, and out in the weather on cold, rainy nights late in the year, I had to do something or I was going to die. I found a one-night-a-week job in a pizza shop in the old Tollgate Mall in Bel Air. The second Saturday I was there I received a strange telephone call. It was from a woman I couldn't remember ever meeting. What she did was a lot like what Jesus had done in the story of the woman at the well (see John 4:1-42). She told me all that I had done, and I knew that God was speaking through her.

She said,"Willie, Father God spoke to me and told me that the pain and sadness you have suffered in this life is too much for you to handle, and that you're about to give up, because you think you're all alone in this world. Well, people may have given up on you, but I'm calling to tell you that God hasn't. He knows your pain and your abandonment. The people who are looking for you can no longer touch you, for He has His hand on you.

"The things you were involved in—the sorcery, the relationships, and other sins—God has forgiven you of all that. It is all under the blood." She was very explicit about it all, naming the things I have just told you about in my story.

While I was on that phone, time seemed to stand still. The sounds in the pizza shop faded into the background, and what I was hearing was that voice. Tears streamed down my face, as I was overcome with emotion, and I dropped the phone, leaving it swinging on its cord.

Then, after a while, I heard, "Willie! Willie!," and I picked the phone up again. "Willie," Darlene said, "just meet me on the corner of Bel Air Road and Tollgate. I'll be in a maroon Ford. My name is Darlene. My husband Dale and I are going to take you into our home to live with us, and you need to come right now."

I don't remember telling my boss that I was leaving that day. I left and met Darlene, and true to their word, she and Dale took me into their home.

That house on Bel Air Road holds so many beautiful, strange, miraculous and joyous memories for me. It was the first time I knew what a real home could be like. I vividly remember us all around the dining room table. Suddenly I had a family that loved me and taught me about life. It would take a whole book to tell of the many people who came to that home and how each of them affected my future.

It was in that house where I celebrated my first Christmas as a believer. Most importantly, God used people I met there to lead me into the baptism in the Holy Ghost, into the healing of my mind and into deliverance from the demons of addiction.

While I lived there, I was able to witness the Gospel to many people, and I continue to do that. As this book goes to press, I have not smoked marijuana or used other chemicals to alter my mental and emotional state in nearly thirty-five years. Jesus set me free.

I am honored that I have been asked to share what I can about my time at the Bel Air home. Of everything, one thing still stands out in my memory: how a woman I had never met could allow God to place His love in her heart for someone she didn't even know and cause her to meet him and become a blessing to him. Mom, I love you and will never forget this miracle as long as I live.

A Word from Tracey Allen

Tracy was that one person I asked God to give me who had made it to recovery from the prison. She writes:

In December of 1982, I was arrested and sent to Towson Detention Center. It was my first time in prison, and I was afraid and wanted to go home. That, however, was not possible.

For me, it was a horrible experience. Then, one Saturday afternoon, a guard announced church service, and I was delighted. Nearly all the women in the prison attended the service, and Darlene was the chaplain. I found her to be a very powerful and, most of all, loving individual. Her husband was there too, and another lady brought a guitar and accompanied the music. That service gave me hope and encouragement to trust God.

I had been raised in a Catholic family and had never felt the power of God before, but when Darlene did the service that day, I could feel His power. That brought me to a belief in God, and I began to depend on those services to get me through the weeks and months ahead. Through them, I learned to trust Jesus. I was an inmate at the Towson prison for only ninety days, but that was enough to be introduced to the Gospel and find God's help for my life.

The day before I was scheduled to go to court, where my fate would be decided, Darlene came to visit me. I had no idea that she was coming. God had sent her to tell me that I would be released and would be going home. She told me something else very important that day on God's behalf: "People, places and things have to change." I knew that God was calling me to a new life.

Praise God for His mercy and grace. Just as she had said, that next day I was released on probation. A month or so after I got back home, I wrote Darlene a letter telling her how well I was doing. Then, in 2004, I decided to call her. What a miracle that she still had the same phone number! I wanted to invite her to my upcoming graduation. I was one of two African-American women to graduate from the Hebrew University in Maryland. Darlene had been my first spiritual mentor, and I wanted her to see the miracle God had done in me. She attended the graduation, along with other mentors who had invested in me and supported me in growing to be a woman of God.

Since then Darlene and I stay in contact with each other, and the Lord has used us to work together in ministry. I want to praise Him for sending her to Towson Detention Center in 1982, for she was used by Him to bring me to the light of Jesus Christ.

Tracey Allen

Author Contact Page

You may contact Darlene Graves directly at her email address:

darlenegraves37@gmail.com

CPSIA information can be obtained
at www.ICGtesting.com
Printed in the USA
FFOW04n0010110516
23944FF

9 781940 461489